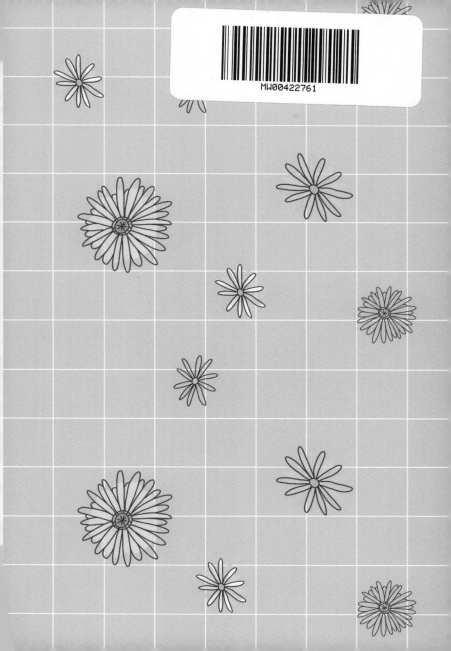

Gilmore girls

the RORY GILMORE

Reading Challenge

THE OFFICIAL GUIDE TO ALL THE BOOKS

Erika Berlin

RUNNING PRESS
PHILADELPHIA

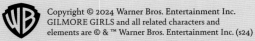

Copyright © 2024 Warner Bros. Entertainment Inc.
GILMORE GIRLS and all related characters and
elements are © & ™ Warner Bros. Entertainment Inc. (s24)

Running Press
Hachette Book Group
1290 Avenue of the Americas, New York, NY 10104
www.runningpress.com
@Running_Press

First Edition: October 2024

Published by Running Press, an imprint of Hachette Book Group, Inc. The Running Press
name and logo are trademarks of Hachette Book Group, Inc.

The Hachette Speakers Bureau provides a wide range of authors for speaking events. To find
out more, go to www.hachettespeakersbureau.com or email HachetteSpeakers@hbgusa.com.

Running Press books may be purchased in bulk for business, educational,
or promotional use. For more information, please contact your local
bookseller or the Hachette Book Group Special Markets Department at
Special.Markets@hbgusa.com.

The publisher is not responsible for websites (or their content)
that are not owned by the publisher.

Print book cover and interior design by Amanda Richmond

Library of Congress Cataloging-in-Publication Data
Names: Berlin, Erika, author.
Title: The Rory Gilmore reading challenge : the official guide to all the books / Erika Berlin.
Other titles: At head of title: Gilmore girls
Description: First edition. | Philadelphia : Running Press, 2024.
Identifiers: LCCN 2024007692 (print) | LCCN 2024007693 (ebook) | ISBN 9780762486649
(hardcover) | ISBN 9780762486656 (ebook)
Subjects: LCSH: Gilmore girls (Television program : 2000-2007)—Miscellanea.
Classification: LCC PN1992.77.G54 B47 2024 (print) | LCC PN1992.77.G54 (ebook) | DDC
791.45/72—dc23/eng/20240229
LC record available at https://lccn.loc.gov/2024007692
LC ebook record available at https://lccn.loc.gov/2024007693

ISBNs: 978-0-7624-8664-9 (hardcover), 978-0-7624-8665-6 (ebook)

Printed in China

APS

10   9   8   7   6   5   4   3   2   1

Contents

Introduction

When *Gilmore Girls* premiered in 2000, the premise was simple: a mother and daughter who were best friends. Lorelai and Rory, two peas living in an idyllic little hamlet pod called Stars Hollow. And while theirs was the core relationship of the show, viewers were further drawn into the multifaceted dynamics of their quirky neighbors, their priggish relatives, Lorelai's outlandish work colleagues, and Rory's cunning classmates. In short, it was a world with innumerable characters that would become a home away from home for years to come.

When we meet Rory for the first time, she's a studious, conscientious teen who already has her life plan plotted out: go to an Ivy League–feeder school, attend Harvard, and become a foreign correspondent like her idol, Christiane Amanpour. From the beginning, Rory was toting around an impressive number of books and casually reading classics that likely weren't on the typical high school sophomore's literature syllabus.

But while Rory may have been a bookworm, she was no wallflower. From the pilot's opening scene through the show's seven-season, 153-episode run, we saw again and again how much of her mother's fierce, fiery independence and biting wit had taken root in her only child. Lorelai and Rory loved hard, fought hard, and opinionated hard. They, like many of the authors Rory admired, showed the world the multifaceted nature of women's lives, ambitions, and aspirations—all while dishing out more words and pop culture references per minute than most any other prime-time show at the time could dream of.

For fans of the show, one of the most dedicated ways to stay in the *Gilmore Girls* world was to commit to one Herculean task: The Rory Gilmore Reading Challenge. In 2014, BuzzFeed published a list of 339 books that an Australian writer had compiled, and *Gilmore Girls* devotees took it and ran. Since then, the list has been read, refined, and discussed, and other bloggers have created their own thoroughly annotated book and episode guides.

This book is a distillation of those zealous inventories. Some overly specific books were cut for obvious reasons. For instance, when Lorelai makes an offhanded reference to a Manson Family member, it doesn't necessarily mean she's read a particular Charles Manson biography—we all glean culture facts from other sources. And when it was unclear if a reference was made to a book or the movie that was made based on the book, it has been included on a separate list. Every effort has been made to be true to the nature of the characters, the context within the show, and the contribution of the original work listed.

And, speaking of the original works, because this book is focused on those books, the publication date listed corresponds to its first book printing. Many stories were originally serialized in journals or magazines first, then published as a whole a couple of years later. Many diaries and collections of works were published decades after they were written. Some ancient works have guesstimated circa dating. However, one exception has been made to this first publication rule: Shakespeare. Many of his plays were written and performed (and therefore publicly consumed) decades before they were officially published, so we've used circa dating to a play's first performance. Again, care was taken to be as accurate as possible.

This is by no means a definitive list, but it is thorough, verified, and more complete than any others we've seen. There are 311 works listed in the official episode guide, in addition to another 96 from referenced authors, 30 Book or Movie? entries, and 177 additional suggested reads; in total, this reading challenge covers 614 possible reads! And while this is still considered a Rory-centric reading list, it's more precisely a Rory-universe reading list. Here we've included books that Lorelai read; books that Rory's most like-minded boyfriend, Jess, carried around in his back pocket; and those her friends like Lane and Paris pored over. Rory swapped book suggestions with her grandfather, and her grandmother belonged to a book club. Hell, even Sookie, Lorelai's bubbly, havoc-wreaking chef of a best friend, read a couple of books!

This reading guide is meant to help you reacquaint yourself with the world of Stars Hollow in a much more intimate way. Whether you choose to start from the very beginning or want to dive into the literary favorites of a particular character, you'll find a guide within. Discussion questions linking the plots of the books to the plots of the show are included, so rewatching various episodes or full seasons along the way is not only helpful but very much encouraged. You'll notice that not every episode has a book reference while some episodes have many—'tis just the nature of storytelling.

And if making any particular part of this challenge a routine feels daunting, take a bit of advice from our bibliophile queen herself: "I just take a book with me everywhere," Rory once said. "It's a habit."

Rory's Essential Reads: The Top Five Books to Better Understand the Heart and Mind of Rory Gilmore

From the beginning, Rory was an insatiable reader who was never without a book (or a half dozen) in her bag. Her need for the written word was perhaps only rivaled by her need for another cup of coffee. And of the many, many books Rory spent time with, waxed poetic about, and piled high on her shelves, these five perhaps spoke to her—and stayed with her—on a different level.

Anna Karenina

(1878) BY LEO TOLSTOY

(SEASON 1, EPISODE 16)

Anna Karenina is the kind of sweeping epic that a reader like Rory could return to again and again and keep finding new ways to analyze. Yes, the primary storyline follows the high-stakes affair between the eponymous heroine and the dashing Count Vronsky, but the interwoven stories of other characters and their relationships explore themes ranging from fidelity and marriage to family and commitment, faith and devotion, and societal expectations and consequences. Which parts do you think sixteen-year-old Rory internalized most? What parts of this novel will stick with you long-term?

While trying to convince Dean to give the book another shot, she explains that Tolstoy wrote for the common man, and although the character names may be a bit difficult to grasp initially, the storylines themselves aren't. Do you agree? What characters or plot devices within the novel do you think were written to be accessible to all?

Novels: 1930–1962
(2 volumes)

BY DAWN POWELL

(SEASON 2, EPISODE 20)

We first see Rory reading Dawn Powell early in season 2, and by the end of the school year, she's rhapsodizing to Lane about how it's a shame no one knows Powell because she "wrote sixteen amazing novels, nine plays, and there are some who actually claim that it was Powell who made the jokes that Dorothy Parker got credit for." ("Blasphemy!" declares Lane; Rory says she won't believe it until she sees proof of Powell's involvement in a smear campaign.) Split between her "Ohio novels" (where Powell was raised) and her "Manhattan novels" (where she was deeply embedded in the Greenwich Village literary scene), Powell's work ranges from melancholic to ebullient—something for any mood. Which of Powell's stories do you think Rory gravitates toward more: the pensive or the cheery?

The Unabridged
Journals of Sylvia Plath
(2000) BY SYLVIA PLATH
(SEASON 1, EPISODE 12)

One of the most memorable visuals of a young Rory engrossed in her reading involves this book—as the camera pans out from the cover of Plath's smiling face, we see sixteen-year-old Rory sitting on a bench in Stars Hollow, Chilton badge on her jacket, hair pushed back by a headband, eyes fully concentrating on the pages and not on her boyfriend, who just walked out of the school across the street. Ah, to be young, carefree, and making jokes about lithium.

"I can never read all the books I want; I can never be all the people I want and live all the lives I want," Plath wrote. Do you think Rory relates to Plath's intellectual grievances like these? If you had significantly more time, what would you spend it on? Books? Hobbies? A second career as a true crime novelist?

Even as a voracious reader and aspiring journalist, we never see or hear about Rory journaling (aside from her mother chiding her in season 5 about her detailed daily diaries—"8 a.m. got up; 8:15 brushed teeth; 8:25 had impure thoughts"). Why do you think that is? Do you find journaling to be helpful? Tedious? Meditative?

While Plath published a number of poems and stories during her life and a volume of her journals was published in 1982, nearly twenty years after her death, this particular *Unabridged Journals* collection was hot off the presses when episode 12 was filmed. The collection was published in October 2000; audiences saw Rory reading it on a park bench in January 2001.

Dead Souls

(1842) BY NIKOLAI VASILYEVICH GOGOL

(SEASON 3, EPISODE 3)

In a perfect example of the dichotomy of Rory's interests, one minute she was swooning over the cheesy perfection of *The Brady Bunch Variety Hour*, but as soon as her application to Harvard arrived in the mail, she bemoaned that just that morning she'd been reading *Dead Souls*. Rory and Lorelai resolve to tell people she was reading the heady Russian novel when her application came, rather than the program *TV Guide* had listed as one of the fifty worst TV shows.

If that concern seems a bit silly or absurd, then perhaps this was the right book for the ruse—in *Dead Souls*, a disgraced government official named Chichikov sets out to acquire dead souls in an odd get-rich-quick scheme.

Going from property to property, he offers to buy the souls (i.e., the legal rights to the dead serfs who were still counted among the estate's assets) so that he can quietly take out a loan against the soul-assets and pocket the earnings. It's absurdist satire, nineteenth-century Russian style at its best.

Which part of this Homeric work did you enjoy the most: the caricatures of the townspeople Chichikov swindles, who each embody some kind of scorn-worthy attribute; or the main character's repeated attempts at chicanery? Does anyone in the large cast of characters remind you of the quirky Stars Hollow townspeople Rory encounters daily?

The Adventures of Huckleberry Finn

(1884) BY MARK TWAIN

(SEASON 1, EPISODE 1)

Huck Finn has been called the Great American Novel, and William Faulkner dubbed Twain the "father of American literature." This book was the very first one mentioned in the series—do you think that's a nod to the importance books will play in Rory's life, or just a coincidence, considering *Huck Finn* has historically been one of the most taught and discussed books in the American curriculum?

Huck Finn also has the honor of being one of the very last literary references in the series—in the antepenultimate episode, Rory reminisces about how she begged to have her twelfth birthday at the Mark Twain House and Museum in Hartford (a real, open-to-the-public place!); Lorelai replied, "I thought one day I was going to find you on a raft made out of milk cartons sailing down the Housatonic River." Did you have similar obsessions as a child? What were some of your favorite books at that age, and did you also playact as the characters?

Ways to Organize Your Book Collection

While Rory's childhood bedroom may have had books in the dresser drawers and in stacks under her bed ("organized chaos" as her grandfather called it), it's safe to assume her adult bookshelves are more thought out. Purely alphabetized bookshelves can feel difficult to browse, but haphazardly stacking books without a system makes it hard to find your treasures. Try one—or all!—of these more instinctual organizing systems.

ORGANIZE BY SUBJECT MATTER

Many people intuitively shelve their cookbooks or travel guides together, but the same concept can work for other popular subject matter. Do you own a more-than-average number of books about the French Revolution, or ghost stories, or books by favorite comedians? Group them together on a shelf, and perhaps add a souvenir Eiffel Tower as a bookend to your French collection or a framed Liz Lemon quote atop the stack of comedic memoirs.

ORGANIZE BY GENRE

Have an outsized collection of science fiction novels that you're always recommending to friends? Or an enviable manga and anime trove? They belong together, and they belong in the part of your living space that best represents them—a shelf of colorful anime spines would look right at home next to any gaming equipment, and if sci-fi is your go-to genre, they could go front-and-center on a living room or den bookshelf.

ORGANIZE BY COLOR

We would never judge a book by its cover, but sometimes a colorful binding can help it find its home amongst a curated rainbow shelf. If visual aesthetics bring you joy, then ROYGBIV those books to your heart's content!

CREATE YOUR OWN "TAKE A BOOK, LEAVE A BOOK" SHELF

Book folk tend to have extras lying around—perhaps you carried the paperback while commuting, but you wanted the hardback for your permanent collection. Or maybe you read and enjoyed a book but decided you didn't *realllly* need to keep it. Pass along the gift of prose to your guests! Not only will your friends appreciate the rotating selection of choices, but you might even become the recipient of a few books you didn't know you needed.

CREATE A CURATED TBR SHELF

That To Be Read pile can be both a blessing and a curse. Keep it under control by reserving a space that can't hold more than, say, one or two dozen books. This will give space for long-term goal reading or that hot new novel everyone's talking about, plus a couple of gift books your fellow bookworms have passed your way.

> VOCAB: *Tsundoku.* A Japanese term used to describe a person who owns a lot of unread literature. It can also refer to a grouping of books that are waiting to be read. If you bought or were gifted this book, you likely are and have *tsundoku*.

How to Maximize Your Reading Time and Become a More Mindful Reader

I ntentionality. Deliberateness. Mindfulness. These aren't just yoga-retreat buzzwords—they're solid practices to improve your mindset, your day-to-day activities, and your attentiveness to your own needs. And they can be applied to your time spent reading as well.

When it comes to settling in with a good book, applying a few mindfulness techniques can help you absorb the material more thoroughly, remember the plot points or new information more accurately, and generally keep you engrossed and engaged longer. To leave passive reading and multitasking reading behind, try these tips:

CHOOSE BOOKS THAT ARE FOR PLEASURE, NOT WORK OR PROFESSIONAL DEVELOPMENT.

This is not to say you shouldn't read career-focused books! But for the sake of practicing mindful reading, you want to find something that activates a different part of your brain than the one that's been buzzing from eight hours of meetings, answering circle-back emails, or prepping for presentations. Start with a dreamy novel, a biography of someone you admire, or some long-form journalism on a topic that will not stress you out.

SLOW DOWN AND APPRECIATE THE TEXT.

There is no need to speed-read, even if you're way behind on this month's book club selection. Take a moment to appreciate the prose, savor a juicy detail, or commit to memory a phrase or quip you could see yourself using in real life. If there's a passage that speaks to you, read it again! Periodically stopping to appreciate what you've read is like stopping to smell the roses—they're both good for you.

HIDE YOUR CELL PHONE.

Seriously. Silence notifications, leave your phone in the other room, take off your smartwatch, become a thirty-minute Luddite. Constant pings from your group chat, email alerts about monthly "semiannual" sales, and app updates are a distraction and a drain on your mental resources. If you want to be present while you read, be *intentional* and ditch your electronics for a few.

TAKE A MOMENT TO REFLECT ON WHAT YOU JUST READ.

Once you're ready to set your book down for the day, pause and remember the parts you just read. Which anecdote will you tell a friend about? What new bit of information did you find particularly fascinating? Did something you just read remind you to look something else up later? By ending your mindful reading session with a brief, personal recap, you're further locking that information away and slowly learning to focus your attention on the present.

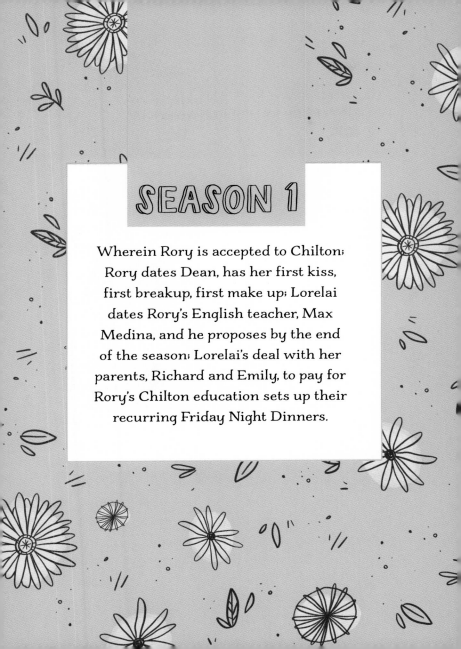

SEASON 1

Wherein Rory is accepted to Chilton; Rory dates Dean, has her first kiss, first breakup, first make up; Lorelai dates Rory's English teacher, Max Medina, and he proposes by the end of the season; Lorelai's deal with her parents, Richard and Emily, to pay for Rory's Chilton education sets up their recurring Friday Night Dinners.

Moby-Dick; or, The Whale
(1851) BY HERMAN MELVILLE

Rory is reading this book ("my first Melville," she says), which she soon finds out Dean already knew because he's been watching her. The allegorical *Moby-Dick* introduced the phrase "searching for [or chasing] the great white whale" into the greater lexicon, meaning a goal one is obsessive about achieving, even to the point of disregarding logic or safety. What do you think Rory's white whale in life is? Lorelai's?

Madame Bovary
(1857) BY GUSTAVE FLAUBERT

While Dean was confessing to noticing Rory and her reading preferences ("After school you come out and you sit under that tree there and you read. Last week it was *Madame Bovary*. This week it's *Moby-Dick*"), we also get a little window into her pre-pilot habits. We're also beginning to learn more about Lorelai and how the mother-daughter pair came to call Stars Hollow home.

In many ways, Lorelai is the exact opposite of Flaubert's protagonist in that she shunned her parents' wealthy lifestyle and society friends rather than running toward it, as Emma Bovary did. Rory is also similarly unimpressed with material things—what do you think she thought of the vain, impetuous Madame Bovary?

Another way to view the character of Madame Bovary is of a woman with such an unattainable definition of happiness that she can never find fulfilment in her romances. Might this be a fair assessment of Lorelai's love life? Where is the line between always wanting more and not settling for less?

"The Little Match Girl"
(1845) BY HANS CHRISTIAN ANDERSEN

After a fight, Rory asks Lorelai if they are going to continue standing outside her grandparents' doorway reenacting "The Little Match Girl" or go inside. Ironically, in the Danish fairy tale, a vision of her grandmother is what makes the little girl so content that she lights all the matches to keep herself warmed by the presence of her grandmother's spirit. Lorelai has made her feelings toward her mother, Emily Gilmore, clear, but do you think Emily ever becomes a true comforting presence for Rory?

TIME FOR CLASS

On Rory's first day of Chilton, during a discussion on the influence of each European culture on modern literature, her teacher points out that although French culture was a dominant influence in Russia, Leo Tolstoy's favorite author was Charles Dickens. As Paris correctly answers, Tolstoy turned to *David Copperfield* in particular for inspiration when writing both *War and Peace* and *Anna Karenina*; Tolstoy once named *Copperfield* as one work that had an "enormous" influence on him and called it a prime example of "universal art."

When you read these books back to back, can you see the influence of Dickens on Tolstoy? Do any of Tolstoy's specific characters or plot points feel explicitly or especially Dickensian? Which author's work do you prefer?

- *War and Peace* (1869) by Leo Tolstoy
- *Anna Karenina* (1878) by Leo Tolstoy
- *David Copperfield* (1850) by Charles Dickens
- *Great Expectations* (1861) by Charles Dickens
- *A Tale of Two Cities* (1859) by Charles Dickens
- *Little Dorrit* (1857) by Charles Dickens

Do you think that Tolstoy was drawn to many of Dickens's works, which famously feature orphans, because he himself was orphaned at age nine?

Bonus Q: Which of these six novels has the best BBC miniseries? Which do you think Rory and Lorelai would regularly binge on movie nights?

The Hunchback of Notre-Dame
(1831) BY VICTOR HUGO

When the Gilmore girls arrive at Chilton for Rory's first day, they sit in their Jeep, staring up at the grotesques on the roof. As Lorelai cranes her neck, she jokes that she's trying to see if there's a hunchback in the bell tower. Hugo's novel is just as much about the cathedral itself and the importance of Paris's Gothic architecture as a whole as it is about Quasimodo, Esmeralda, and the rest of her suitors. Rory tends to have a similar love for great, hallowed halls, such as Chilton, Harvard, and Yale. Do you like spending time studying beautiful old architecture, like those at colleges and churches? Which part of the book did you enjoy more—the character plots or the vivid imagery of nineteenth-century Paris?

A Mencken Chrestomathy
(1948) BY H. L. MENCKEN

One of the things Rory and her grandfather quickly bonded over was their love of reading, and the works of H. L. Mencken were among the first that they discussed. Mencken as a cultural critic was known for his satire, acerbic wit, and cynicism, and this collection includes segments from books of his like *In Defense of Women* and *Notes on Democracy*, and musings on everyone from Woodrow Wilson, the Roosevelts, Walt Whitman, Nietzsche, Beethoven, and Rudolph Valentino. But really, who do you think would enjoy this book most: Rory, Richard, or Paris?

> VOCAB: *Chrestomathy*. A volume of selected passages or stories of an author.

The Days [3 volumes]
(1947) BY H. L. MENCKEN

Richard, a collector of biographies, surprises Rory by telling her he found a first edition of this set of Mencken's memoirs. As a famed journalist, it makes sense that Mencken's life and work would pique Rory's interest. During her time at the *Franklin* and again at the *Yale Daily News*, do you think any of Mencken's often inflammatory but always cocksure takes seeped into Rory's writing? (For example, her critique of the ballerina or of Logan's networking event.)

Mencken's career was defined not just for his journalistic contributions but also for his extensive influence in literary circles (he famously published early works by F. Scott Fitzgerald, Joseph Conrad, and James Joyce). Considering Rory's love of literature, do you think following a similar career trajectory—starting in journalism and pivoting into book publishing—would be satisfying for her? Why or why not?

Peyton Place

(1956) BY GRACE METALIOUS

When Richard refers to the scandalous behavior of various members of his country club as being very *Peyton Place*, Rory doesn't bat an eye. Most of the "scandals" in Stars Hollow were along the lines of Taylor Doose creating another annoying rule, or that a certain innkeeper and diner proprietor were on (or off) again. Has any truly scandalous event happened in your hometown?

A SHAKESPEAREAN STUDY SESH

——◇◇◇◇◇——

As Rory panics about an upcoming test in Mr. Medina's class, Lorelai tries to help her study. With a comprehensive Shakespearean guide draped over the arm of the couch and a bag of potato chips in her arms, Rory focuses on memorizing the dates that these works were written or published (for example, *The Comedy of Errors* was written in the 1590s but not published until 1623), and which of the sonnets are in iambic pentameter (all but Sonnet 145, which is written in tetrameter). While many of us focused on similar information for our high school tests, do you remember any of those specifics now? Looking back, what do you wish you'd learned more about regarding the classics?

> In many ways, *Gilmore Girls* is one ongoing comedy of errors. If Miss Patty staged a performance of one of the Bard's plays, who (besides Kirk) would be cast?

- *Who's Who and What's What in Shakespeare* (1987) by Evangeline O'Connor
- *The Comedy of Errors* (c. 1590s) by William Shakespeare
- *Richard III* (1597) by William Shakespeare
- *The Sonnets* (1609) by William Shakespeare

SONNET 116

Let me not to the marriage of true minds
Admit impediments. Love is not love
Which alters when it alteration finds,
Or bends with the remover to remove.
O no! it is an ever-fixed mark
That looks on tempests and is never shaken;
It is the star to every wand'ring bark,
Whose worth's unknown, although his height be taken.

Paris menacingly recites this portion of Sonnet 116 to Rory before adding, "You're going down." Why do you think she chose this sonnet to intimidate Rory with? It is usually read as a rumination on the nature of true love—how might Paris be interpreting the poem?

A Room of One's Own
(1929) BY VIRGINIA WOOLF

We see Rory reading this book on the bus—she's often able to create at least a mental space of her own while reading. This extended essay was based on two lectures Woolf gave at women's colleges. One of the points she purposefully makes while speaking to rooms full of women who had the opportunity to pursue formal education in the way that many centuries-worth of women were never able to was that because men historically wrote both the history and the fiction, their portrayal was always subject to the whims of men.

> *"Imaginatively she is of the highest importance; practically she is completely insignificant. She pervades poetry from cover to cover; she is all but absent from history. She dominates the lives of kings and conquerors in fiction; in fact she was the slave of any boy whose parents forced a ring upon her finger. Some of the most inspired words and profound thoughts in literature fall from her lips; in real life she could hardly read; scarcely spell; and was the property of her husband."*

Do you think this lesson is still relevant today? Which portrayals of women in classic literature do you think would have been more interesting or well-rounded if written by a woman? Do you think *Gilmore Girls* and its many strong female characters resonated so well because it was created by a woman and so many of its writing team were women?

Piggybacking off of this idea, Woolf's most famous assertion was that societal patriarchy has been to the detriment of women's personal artistic and intellectual achievements. There are many men throughout this book list who benefitted greatly from having wives who were sidelined to roles of domesticity, as Woolf describes (consider the time men like Shakespeare and Dickens were able to devote to their craft and the fame and fortune it brought them, and compare that to the ways their wives were treated). Do you think this resonates with Rory, who wants to be a journalist and knows she needs that time to focus on her work? Do you think these ideas follow her through any of her relationships?

The Crucible

(1953) BY ARTHUR MILLER

As Stars Hollow overdecorates for Thanksgiving and Rory and Lane are manning a Cornucopia Can Drive dressed as pilgrims, Lorelai makes a crack that Luke would look good "dressed like the guys from *The Crucible*" when he rejects Taylor's demands that he participate as well. Of course, this would mean some seventeenth-century knee-length breeches and stockings to emulate the costumes from Miller's Tony-winning play about the Salem Witch Trials (even though Miller wrote the play, which was based on real events and people, as an allegory for the extremely witch-hunt-esque McCarthyism of the 1950s). Does your community have a resident Taylor and/or Luke? Which are you when it comes to participating in local events?

> FUN FACT: Did you know that Connecticut had its own detrimental witch trials based in Hartford, which predated the infamous Salem ones by thirty years?

CHOOSE YOUR OWN READING ADVENTURE

——◇◇◇◇◇——

Early on in their relationship, a completely smitten Rory and Dean trade book recommendations as often as kisses in the grocery aisle. In one quick bus-stop conversation, Dean reluctantly admits he liked one of Rory's Jane Austen suggestions, and when Rory gloats to Lane, Dean tells her she needs to read Hunter S. Thompson. Rory counters with Charlotte Brontë. Dean goes in for a kiss. Lane looks visibly ill.

If the key to knowing a person's mind is through their bookshelf, which selection of each of these authors' works do you think Rory and/or Dean would most relate to?

JANE AUSTEN

- *Pride and Prejudice* (1813)
- *Sense and Sensibility* (1811)
- *Emma* (1815)

CHARLOTTE BRONTË

- *Jane Eyre* (1847)
- *Shirley* (1849)
- *Villette* (1853)

HUNTER S. THOMPSON

- *Fear and Loathing in Las Vegas* (1971)
- *Hell's Angels: The Strange and Terrible Saga of the Outlaw Motorcycle Gangs* (1967)
- *The Rum Diary* (1998)

The Group
(1963) BY MARY McCARTHY

This bestseller follows the Depression-era lives of eight affluent Vassar girls after they graduate and try to make their way in the world. These highly educated friends are each beset by a myriad of problems—sexism in the workplace, cheating husbands, raising children—all while trying to live the lives they thought they would be entitled to upon graduation. Which of the eight women might Rory understand the best? Which do you relate to? Do you see any of the struggles your friends or family have had in the stories of these women?

Thirty years after McCarthy's book hit it big, a New York editor told a popular columnist to create something like *The Group*—what resulted was Candace Bushnell's column and subsequent book, *Sex and the City*. Which of these two juicy reads do you think Rory would prefer? What about Lorelai? Or Madeline and Louise?

The Portable Dorothy Parker

(1944) BY DOROTHY PARKER

Parker was a poet and satirist who sat at the center of New York's most prestigious literary circle, but while her shrewd, sardonic commentary makes for an amusing read, this particular tome also contains numerous (killjoy) tales about relationships, marriages, and short-lived romances (awkward that Rory and Dean lose track of time reading this book on the night they officially cement their relationship status!). Why do you think Rory is drawn to Parker's work? What do you like or dislike about Parker's writing?

> FUN FACT: Parker's famed wit and wordplay had an outsized influence on *Gilmore Girls* show creator Amy Sherman-Palladino, who named her production studio Dorothy Parker Drank Here Productions.

The Metamorphosis
(1915) BY FRANZ KAFKA

"I think it *is* romantic!" Rory asserts when Lane questions why she bought this particular, odd little novella as a Christmas gift for Dean. Kafka's most famous work is an allegory of the effects personal and societal alienation can have on an individual, and is more often read as surrealist horror or as absurdist tragicomedy. Why do you think Rory picked *The Metamorphosis* as a gift for Dean rather than just recommending it? Who would you gift this book to?

The Miracle Worker
(1959) BY WILLIAM GIBSON

Whether Rory referenced the Tony-winning play or the Academy Award–winning movie ("Things are still very *Miracle Worker* at my house," she tells Lane when asked if she and her mother had made up after a rift), this story of a teacher, Anne Sullivan, and her world-famous pupil, Helen Keller, is an important cultural touchstone. Do you think the film would be in Lorelei and Rory's movie night rotation?

Swann's Way
(1913) BY MARCEL PROUST

This is the first book of Proust's seven-volume novel *In Search of Lost Time*, and one *actually* considered to be extremely romantic (sorry, Rory). Do you think Max was pleased when Lorelai picked this book off his shelf? What other books might a literature teacher want to give a newish paramour?

Swann's Way is the work in which Proust's "madeleine episode" scene coined the phrase "involuntary memory"—that is, when some current sensory experience suddenly transports an individual to a long-past memory. What kind of madeleine does *Gilmore Girls* bring to you? Do certain people or places instantly remind you of your friends in Stars Hollow?

The Poems of Emily Dickinson
(1955) BY EMILY DICKINSON

After Mr. Medina quotes the first stanza of an 1861 Dickinson poem, he encourages the class to appreciate how convincingly she could write about passion and the world even while living as a virtual recluse. Madeline then quips to Louise that she could "listen to him talk about passion all day." Who would you want to hear recite Emily Dickinson poetry?

THERE'S A CERTAIN SLANT OF LIGHT, (320)
There's a certain Slant of light
Winter Afternoons—
That oppresses, like the Heft
Of Cathedral Tunes—

Carrie

(1974) BY STEPHEN KING

As Rory works to befriend Paris, Madeline, and Louise, she quips that they've moved on from "the plan to dump the pig's blood on me at prom." Of all the cruel things Paris has said and done to Rory, do you think she'd stage a prank as straightforward as this? Who else in the Chilton universe might be capable of it? Have you ever witnessed a prank as sinister as the *Carrie* one? What's the worst prank you've ever seen pulled?

A Streetcar Named Desire
(1947) BY TENNESSEE WILLIAMS

Lorelai loves a *Streetcar* reference! After Rory brought home a live class-project bird, Lorelai named it Stanley, and then switched it to Stella when she's told it's a female bird. You probably guessed what would come next—Lorelai proceeds to lose the bird and shouts *"Stellllllaaaaa!"* What do you think of Lorelai's animal naming conventions for this bird and her dog, Paul Anka? What are some of your favorite pet names that you have either used yourself or have heard used?

Gone With the Wind
(1936) BY MARGARET MITCHELL

When Paris refers to the girl Tristan is brazenly making out with as Belle Watling, she's referring to the Atlanta brothel madam who has a long-standing relationship with Rhett Butler. Do you think teens today would understand this reference? Did *you* get it? What other literary characters might have felt more contemporary to cite?

A FULL SET OF ILLUSTRATED ENCYCLOPEDIAS

While enjoying a lovely three-month-anniversary dinner with Dean, Rory exclaims, "This is just like that Christmas when I got a full set of illustrated encyclopedias!" ("I wanted them," she quickly clarified.)

But which set did Rory own? The most solid contender seems to be the twenty-volume Golden Book Encyclopedia set from 1988. Various versions had been in print for decades, but the 1988 edition added four volumes, and some supermarket chains such as Acme—a popular regional chain that was widespread in Connecticut—used the set as a promotional deal for shoppers. Would a strapped single mom with a daughter who needed to look up everything from antiseptic to the Milky Way to the Ozark Mountains to *The Wizard of Oz* cash in her points from buying coffee canisters and breakfast cereal in bulk to give a fully illustrated encyclopedia set as a Christmas gift? All signs point to yes.

Nancy Drew 33: The Witch Tree Symbol
(1955) BY CAROLYN KEENE

Lorelai flippantly asserts her detective credentials by saying she's read every Nancy Drew book, including "that one in Amish country twice." (This would be that one, when Nancy tries tracking down a thief in Pennsylvania Dutch Country, but the locals believe she's a witch.) But do you think Lorelai actually has a point—that reading mysteries and solving puzzles can help develop critical thinking and comprehension skills in young adults? What other kinds of skills might early YA mystery series like Nancy Drew, the Hardy Boys, and Encyclopedia Brown help kids learn?

The Art of Eating
(1954) BY M. F. K. FISHER

Mary Frances Kennedy Fisher was a lauded food writer who could write as elegantly about a dish or meal as *Vogue* could about a vintage Chanel. But as much as the Gilmores love food, no one would mistake them for foodies. Do you think Rory was able to appreciate the content of this book as much as the prose? What foods do you think she might write about?

Glengarry Glen Ross
(1983) BY DAVID MAMET

During Emily's rant about all the awful gifts her mother-in-law, Lorelai the First (a.k.a Trix), has given her over the years, Lorelai quips that Mamet must have stopped by. While this Pulitzer-winning play shows the lengths desperate real estate agents will go to unload bad property, it also highlights the skills one must have to convince people they want something they really don't. Who in the *Gilmore Girls* universe do you think has this talent? Who in your own life has this ability?

Hamlet
(c. 1600) BY WILLIAM SHAKESPEARE

When Lorelai's grandmother, Trix, tries to shame her for asking Richard and Emily to pay for Rory's education, she says "You know Shakespeare once wrote, 'Neither a borrower nor a lender be.'" In the play, the king's advisor, Polonius, tells this to his son, along with other platitudes. Polonius, however, is a pompous, hypocritical old wind bag—something Emily certainly thinks is true of her mother-in-law. Do you think this is sound advice? How does it feel hearing not-terrible advice from someone you don't respect?

The Grapes of Wrath
(1939) BY JOHN STEINBECK

Emily takes one look in Lorelai's sparsely stocked fridge and tells Rory it's like *The Grapes of Wrath*. The Pulitzer-winning novel follows the hardworking Joad family as they attempt to migrate during the joint hardships of the Depression and Dust Bowl. Do you think Emily's characterization is correct? (Lorelai does work hard, but unlike the Joads, she has plenty of money for food.) What do you think Emily, who has a full household of ever-rotating help and has never known poverty, would consider a bare minimum to stock a fridge with?

James Joyce's Ulysses: A Study
(1930) BY STUART GILBERT

Joyce's 1922 novel is one of the longest, most notoriously difficult classics out there, so it's not surprising that Rory would read Gilbert's Joyce-approved study (either along with or after reading *Ulysses* itself) instead of a basic CliffsNotes version. Do you think it's ever acceptable to only read an analysis or guide rather than the original text? What if the author had the originator's blessing and help, as Gilbert did of Joyce, with whom he became close friends?

Out of Africa
(1937) BY ISAK DINESEN

Dinesen is the pen name of Karen Blixen, a Danish writer who moved to British East Africa (now Kenya) to marry a Swedish baron and run a six-thousand-acre coffee plantation in the 1910s. *Out of Africa* is a memoir of her seventeen years living there. The young Rory thought the book and Dinesen were "amazing," and the memoir was later turned into a Best Picture–winning movie. The book, however, is now viewed more harshly in light of its romanticized colonialism. What were your thoughts while reading this book? Would a more well-rounded view of the world make this book easier or harder to read in context? What merits does Dinesen's work maintain?

A COMPANION READ

Considering the very white-centric narration of *Out of Africa*, a noteworthy companion read such as Chinua Achebe's acclaimed 1958 novel *Things Fall Apart* could act as a cultural counterweight. Achebe follows a family and village in Nigeria both before and after the European occupation of the continent, known as the Scramble for Africa, in the late nineteenth century. How does the language in these two books differ when discussing native people, colonizers, the land, and the various cultures at play? Do you think companion reads are an important way to get a more thorough understanding of events, or do you think each work should be judged on its own merits?

"The Art of Fiction"

(1884) BY HENRY JAMES

Mr. Medina recommends this essay to his class, calling it a "remarkable manifesto that contains basic truths that still apply to fiction in any form." After discussing types of art and writing, James concludes that "the only condition that I can think of attaching to the composition of the novel is . . . that it be interesting." Do you agree? Even for novels that have a higher purpose of educating or bringing awareness to larger conversations? If they are dull, will they get their point across? Which novels have you found most engrossing?

SEASON 2

Wherein Rory is in her junior year at Chilton; Lorelai abruptly breaks up with Max right before their wedding; Luke's nephew, Jess, comes to live with him; Jess and Rory connect over their love of reading, causing Dean to become extremely jealous and insecure; Lorelai and Luke fight over Jess's influence on Rory; Richard involuntarily retires and then starts his own business soon after; Lorelai and Christopher briefly reunite, but when he discovers his estranged ex is pregnant, he returns to her; Rory kisses Jess.

Secrets of the Flesh: A Life of Colette

(1999) BY JUDITH THURMAN

This biography of the French author, actress, and rumor mill–fodder It Girl Sidonie-Gabrielle Colette, best known as the mononymous Colette, is the kind of juicy profile both Rory and Lorelai would appreciate—Rory for Colette's massive success as the author of the early-century *Claudine* novels (and Colette's subsequent battle to be published under her own name and earn a living with her writing), and Lorelai for her scandalous affairs and knack for continually reinventing herself. Which part of Colette's life did you find the most interesting?

> BONUS READ: Colette's four *Claudine* novels, published between 1900 and 1903, were the talk of Paris.

A Connecticut Yankee in King Arthur's Court

(1889) BY MARK TWAIN

Poor Lane. She likes Henry, a smart, handsome Korean boy (who plans to go to med school!) that her exacting mother would likely approve of, but Lane is too scared to tell her mom about him. Then, seemingly out of nowhere, her parents buy her a one-way ticket to Korea for the summer. While an overly anxious Lane views this as a personal attack, her first-generation mother likely sees it as an important opportunity to stay connected to her heritage and bond with her cousins. Lane becomes resigned to her fate as "A Connecticut Yankee in Busan."

Lane may seem overly dramatic, but the reference was funny, and apt. Just like Twain's protagonist, Hank Morgan, found himself suddenly transported from nineteenth-century Connecticut to King Arthur's medieval court,Lane found herself transported to a world that, though not completely foreign, was certainly unlike her small-town life in Stars Hollow. Have you ever dreaded going on a trip, only to enjoy your time during it?

Elmer Gantry
(1927) BY SINCLAIR LEWIS

"What is love? It is the morning and evening star." While this abbreviated line that Rory pulled as a possible quote for her mother's wedding invitations sounds sweet, it's actually from the highly satirical novel that follows a narcissistic, womanizing salesman who, after having been kicked out of a Baptist seminary, decides to become a traveling evangelist. Knowing Lorelai's general disdain for saccharine sentimentality, what kind of quote would you have suggested to her to use?

> FUN FACT: Lewis notably dedicated this novel to H. L. Mencken, another acerbic author that Rory loves.

The Gospel According to Jesus Christ
(1991) BY JOSÉ SARAMAGO

This book by Nobel-winning Portuguese author José Saramago was lying on the coffee table as Lorelai and Rory watch a movie with Max just before their wedding.

 The fictionalized reimagining of Jesus's life was both praised for being philosophical and slammed by the Vatican as being anti-religious.

Who do you think this book belonged to: Rory, Lorelai, or Max?

The Optimist's Daughter
(1972) BY EUDORA WELTY

The protagonist of this Pulitzer Prize–winning story is a cautious, dutiful daughter who cares for her ailing father while dealing with his self-centered, impudent second wife. Metaphorically, the story is about vision, both physically being able to see but also being able to understand the people and circumstances around you. We see Rory engrossed in this book when her mother (who is often quite the optimist), bursts in to tell her to pack her bags for a road trip. Rory immediately sees what is happening—her mother is now a runaway bride and has created the diversion of a road trip to avoid having to confront Max or her own feelings about the wedding. Do you think Rory identifies with Laurel, the protagonist, who is reserved and contemplative? Do you think she fully understands her mother's decision to hit the road?

Mrs. Dalloway
(1925) BY VIRGINIA WOOLF

This modernist novel follows a day in the life of Mrs. Dalloway, a talkative woman described as the life of the party, who spends her day thinking about the man she *didn't* marry. We see Rory reading this on the couch while Lorelai and Emily argue about the no-longer-necessary wedding gift Emily got Lorelai and Max. Do you think Lorelai and Emily picking a petty fight was their way of avoiding talking about their real emotions, in much the way Mrs. Dalloway glossed over her unhappiness? Have you, or someone you know, called off a wedding? How often do you or they think about what might have been, the way Mrs. Dalloway does?

HOW TO BRANCH OUT OF YOUR LITERARY COMFORT ZONES

―⊸◦◇◦⊷―

"I've read, like, three hundred books in my entire life and I'm already sixteen. Do you know how long it would take me to read thirteen million books?!"

While the Gilmore girls take a campus tour of Rory's dream college, Harvard, Lorelai narrates from a guidebook that the institution, which has the largest academic library in the world, holds more than thirteen million volumes in more than ninety different libraries. Rory's immediate response? "I'm a failure!"

As Rory sees it, in order to converse intelligently with all of the other brainy kids she wants to meet in college, she'll need to read "at least a few from every genre and subgenre."

Her fear that she's been "frittering away" her whole life is clearly unfounded—within a few scenes, she's actively participating in a lecture hall discussion about Seneca and the values of stoicism just as passionately as she discusses pizza toppings or Chinese food menus.

- *Tuesdays with Morrie* (1997) by Mitch Albom
- *Who Moved My Cheese?* (1998) by Spencer Johnson
- *Letters from a Stoic* (c. CE 65) by Lucius Annaeus Seneca

> Lorelai's correct that Rory probably doesn't need to read *Tuesdays with Morrie* or *Who Moved My Cheese?* to make a great impression, but it is helpful that she was well-versed in Seneca before that lecture! Take comfort in knowing there's no way any one person can be fully omnilegent. The happiest readers recognize these limits, even while trying to consume as much as they can.

> **VOCAB:** *Omnilegent.* Reading or having read everything.

But, if you, like Rory, want to branch out of your literary comfort zones, try these tips and tricks:

ASK A BROADER GROUP FOR RECOMMENDATIONS

What are our social networks for if not for social networking? While we all likely discuss and recommend books to our immediate group of friends and family, posting online that you're on the hunt for some new reads is a surefire way to get some more eclectic options from that kid you sat next to in chemistry or the fellow assistant at your first job. And, if publicly posting for advice sounds daunting, you can always scroll through #BookTok for an endless stream of beautifully curated options.

ASK A LIBRARIAN

Shocker: Librarians love talking about books! Many libraries have librarian-curated recommendation lists both online and in-house, and they will often cater them to holidays and events. Major libraries around the world also frequently post recommendation lists online, so browsing their sites will give you a range to choose from.

FIND A CULTURALLY SIGNIFICANT
TOUCHSTONE YOU'VE MISSED

Say you're well-versed in the music, art, and general culture of the 1980s—but have you read the books that helped shape that culture? Like, say, Alice Walker's Pulitzer-winning *The Color Purple* (1982), or Tom Wolfe's behemoth *The Bonfire of the Vanities* (1987). Pick a decade and find out which books were bestsellers, award-winners, and most talked about by the literati.

IDENTIFY A BRAND-NEW-TO-YOU GENRE

Perhaps you've never read a western before! Or any magical realism. Or—gasp!—a dystopian YA series. If you're new to a genre, finding a book by one of its most famous representatives (say, Cormac McCarthy, Isabel Allende) is a good place to start.

FIND OUT WHAT YOUR FAVORITE
WRITERS, MUSICIANS, ETC. ARE READING

Loved Greta Gerwig's latest movie? Google "Greta Gerwig's favorite books," and you'll find plenty of recommendations by her, including books by George Eliot, Elif Batuman, and Elizabeth Bowen. And Gerwig's not the only creative who likes to discuss her favorite literature! Oprah and Reese Witherspoon famously have stickers they attach to their favorite books, but everyone from

Shonda Rhimes to Jimmy Fallon hosts their own online book clubs as well. In addition, the site Radical Reads creates curated reading lists for a wide range of famous readers based on works they discussed at length; luminaries featured include John Lewis, Kehinde Wiley, Diane von Furstenberg, Yara Shahidi, and Bruce Lee.

Finding books that are outside of your comfort zone is the only way you'll find new arenas to love (or loathe, which could be fun too!). For, as Rory told Paris when she was arguing with Jess about the noteworthiness of his beloved Beats writers, "You could say they exposed you to a world you wouldn't have otherwise known—isn't that what great writing's all about?"

The Mojo Collection: The Ultimate Music Companion

(2001) BY JIM IRVIN

As part of Lane's musical education journey, she snagged a just-released copy of the influential British music magazine *Mojo*'s colossal guide to seven decades' worth of popular music. She's focused in on the 1960s: Charles Mingus, The Sonics, MC5, Fairport Convention, and *Odessa* by the Bee Gees (considered a masterpiece of their pre-disco, pre-worldwide-takeover days). Which of these artists do you think ultimately influenced Lane the most?

Selected Letters of Dawn Powell (1913–1965)

(1999) BY DAWN POWELL

This is the first time we see Rory reading Dawn Powell, and we'll soon find out just how much she admires the acerbic writer when she laments that Powell isn't better known. It's been posited that Powell's "relative obscurity was likely due to a general distaste for her harsh satiric tone"—how do you think her writing compares to that of other famous sharp-tongued authors? Do you think that assessment fair, or incomplete? Were other writers with a "harsh satiric tone" relegated to the back of the metaphorical bookshelf, as Powell seems to have been?

The Brothers Karamazov
(1880) BY FYODOR DOSTOEVSKY

Another of the great Russian novels, Mr. Medina has this book stacked on his desk with others he has assigned (meaning Rory has definitely already read it). Famed thinkers like Sigmund Freud called this book "the most magnificent novel ever written," and Albert Einstein once told a fellow writer and scientist that he considered *The Brothers Karamazov* "the supreme summit of all literature." Do you agree? Where does it rank for you among the other Russian literature titles on this list? With the other books, regardless of origin?

Howl and Other Poems
(1956) BY ALLEN GINSBURG

Jess nonchalantly tells Rory he "doesn't read much" and declines when she offers him this collection of "great" Beat poetry. What parts of the poem do you think Rory liked best? And do you think this was a school assignment or one she chose on her own?

Come to find out, Jess views "much" as a relative term—he's read *Howl* about forty times and has left Rory a bunch of marginalia. Considering *Howl* is a rant against conformity, what can we begin to assume about Jess, based on how many times he has returned to and deeply thought about this poem?

VOCAB: *Marginalia.* Writing notes in the margins of books. Jess does this, and, as Rory explains to her mom, "People like Mark Twain wrote in the margins."

Oliver Twist
(1838) BY CHARLES DICKENS

Perplexed by Jess, Rory calls him "Dodger" as she walks off with her returned book. She teases him to figure out the reference, which he immediately does. The Artful Dodger, of course, is the wily pickpocket who befriends the naïve, idealistic Oliver. Does this seem fitting? And which song from the Tony- and Oscar-winning score of *Oliver!* do you think Rory might have hummed to herself on the way home? Do you "Consider Yourself" (. . . figure it out, wink wink) more a fan of the book or the musical?

Who's Afraid of Virginia Woolf?
(1962) BY EDWARD ALBEE

As Richard and Emily bicker on the stairwell, Lorelai refers to them as George and Martha, the verbally cruel couple in Albee's Tony-winning play. When it first came out, the play and subsequent movie were praised for smashing the societal expectations of a perfect American family in a very anti-*Donna Reed* kind of way. Do you think *Gilmore Girls* breaks expectations on what a perfect American family should look like? How so, or not?

THE COMPACT OXFORD
ENGLISH DICTIONARY (1991)

Every reader or writer needs a dictionary on hand, and if you're Rory Gilmore, you'd only covet the best. The *Oxford English Dictionary (OED)* is famously thorough—not only does it have some half-million words and phrases, but it includes both present-day and the complete history of individual words, some dating back centuries.

When the first *Compact OED* was released in 1971, it was astounding. Twenty volumes of the dictionary were condensed into one oversized binding. The *OED* was not abridged; it was photo-reduced—nine pages from the original were fit into one page of the *Compact*. Perhaps anticipating eyesight issues, each boxed copy comes with a magnifying glass.

During season 1, Christopher attempted to buy this for Rory as a grand, fatherly gesture (or, really, to make up for his lack of presence in her everyday life), but his card was declined. That was embarrassing, but this isn't some ten-dollar pocket dictionary—this eighteen-pound leviathan will set you back around five hundred dollars. (A *bargain*, honestly.)

If that's a little rich for your reference book budget, check out your local public or university library's online system. Many have access, and it would be far cheaper (and better for your back) than lugging this beaut around.

Memoirs of a Dutiful Daughter
(1958) BY SIMONE DE BEAUVOIR

Rory stays up late, curled up on the couch with this childhood memoir of the trailblazing French existentialist and early feminist theorist. De Beauvoir describes growing up in a devoutly Catholic bourgeois family but eventually having a crisis of faith and spending her life as an atheist. She describes this break and others as a young woman trying to create her own path in life without disrespecting or alienating her parents along the way. What, if any, stories of de Beauvoir's do you think Rory might identify with? As a dutiful daughter herself, Rory has yet to have any of the major fights with her mother that will come as she starts making her own choices—do you think she actively tries to avoid the same types of fights that broke Lorelai apart from her parents? Have you or someone you know navigated a similar split from family for belief-based reasons? How did that make you feel?

Savage Beauty: The Life of Edna St. Vincent Millay

(2001) BY NANCY MILFORD

This biography of the famed American poet—the first woman to win a Pulitzer for poetry—also talks about the deep love and closeness of the three Millay sisters and their single mother, who filled their home with classic books and gave her daughters the freedom to explore their interests and express themselves creatively. Do you think Rory would read passages or detail specific stories from this and other books to her mother the way the Millay sisters did? What kind of creative pursuits do you share with your parental figures? If you have children, what do they share with you?

The Sound and the Fury

(1929) BY WILLIAM FAULKNER

Once, William Faulkner was asked what he would say to people who complained that his writing was too difficult to understand, even after two or three reads; "Read it four times," he replied. Faulkner works are notoriously dense, difficult, and often have confusing timelines and jumps between narrators. *The Sound and the Fury* is a prime example of this. The novel traces the decline and corruption of one formerly prominent Southern family, the Compsons, and is all based around a line from *Macbeth*—"it is a tale/ Told by an idiot, full of sound and fury/Signifying nothing." How do you think the Compson characters align with Shakespeare's? Are they tragedies on similar scales?

The Last Empire: Essays 1992–2000

(2001) BY GORE VIDAL

This collection of essays from the postmodernist writer focused his acerbic observations on all things American, from the Bill of Rights to the CIA to the Clintons to civil liberties. These pieces were written between the years of Bill Clinton's first presidential campaign through the electoral crisis of 2000 (all pre-9/11) and may have informed Rory's view of the United States and its politics. Do you think Vidal's assessments of Hillary Clinton—he was a longtime supporter of hers—were of particular interest to Rory, considering her admiration of the then-senator? What were your thoughts about that era when reading about it in this way?

The Collected Stories of Eudora Welty
(1980) BY EUDORA WELTY

Welty's talent for writing from numerous perspectives and for crafting "deceptively simple" stories, as the *New Yorker* wrote, are all on display in these forty-one works. This is the second Welty book we've seen Rory work through this season, and later on she will talk about how Welty was one of the writers Lorelai introduced her to. Welty once wrote of her own childhood that "I learned from the age of two or three that any room in our house, at any time of day, was there to read in, or to be read to," and that her mother read to her constantly. Do you think Rory feels a special connection to Welty because of this shared experience? Did you read a lot as a child?

THE SECRET
TO READING MULTIPLE
BOOKS AT ONCE

———◦◇◇◇◦———

Rory had the right idea in this episode when she explained to her exasperated mother why she needed four extra (presumably non-classroom-assigned) books shoved into her already overstuffed backpack. She has a bus book (Edna St. Vincent Millay), another bus book (William Faulkner)—see, one is a biography and the other is a novel, so if she pulls out the biography and isn't feeling it at the moment, she can switch to the novel; *duh!*—a lunch book (Gore Vidal, essays, totally different than a biography or novel), and one more (Eudora Welty, short stories) *justtttt* in case.

That might be a lot to tote around on any given day, but Rory's system is solid. Reading books of varying genres and formats (i.e., a biography, a novel, essays, and short stories) can help your brain keep the stories compartmentalized, thereby making sure the information you absorb is remembered. Other tips for reading and retaining more than one book at a time include:

KEEP THE GENRES AS DIFFERENT AS POSSIBLE
While having one fiction and one nonfiction book going simultaneously is not a bad plan, reading two set in the

same place and time frame—like, say, the nonfiction *Warwick the Kingmaker* (2007) by British medieval historian A. J. Pollard; and *The Kingmaker's Daughter* (2012) by historical fiction doyenne Philippa Gregory—could really muddle not only the storylines but result in your confusing the fact with the fiction.

DIVERSIFY THE FORMATS

While few things beat holding a book and physically turning its pages, we refuse to be snobbish about the incredible gift that is ebooks and audiobooks. If you keep a hardback by your bedside, a digital read for your commute or lunch hour, and an audiobook going while you walk the dog or do more mindless housework (we're looking at you, baskets of laundry!), then you'll have three distinct mediums to help distinguish your current reads.

TAKE NOTES

Remember marginalia? It's not just a quirk—it's science! Writing and memorization have long gone hand in hand; when you make the effort to write your thoughts and observations in the margins of a book, your long-term memory kicks up a notch. A 2021 study of Japanese university students found that after writing on physical paper (i.e., not adding to your notes app or scribbling on a tablet), the brain showed stronger activity when participants

were asked to recall the information an hour later. Plus, not only will you better remember the reading material in the long term, but you can easily refer back to important points in earlier chapters in the short term.

MIX UP THE READING LEVELS

Ever had the urge to go back and reread books from your childhood? Or pick up a hot YA book that you know your nieces and nephews are reading? Do it! Not only will the language and style differ from any of the more adult books you have going, but your *mindset* will be different too. Trust us, you won't confuse Betty Ren Wright's *The Dollhouse Murders* (1983) or any of R. L. Stine's ubiquitous Goosebumps books with anything by Stephen King or Silvia Moreno-Garcia.

"Snow-White and Rose-Red"
(1812) BY BROTHERS GRIMM

When Francie and the other Puffs attempt to deny the existence of the Chilton secret society, they claim it's just folklore, "like Snow-white and Rose-red," or "Mariah Carey's crackup." But this particular fairy tale, even though it was one collected by Wilhelm and Jacob Grimm, is less well-known and not the same as the *Snow White and the Seven Dwarfs* tale that American children know. Why do you think the show's writers decided to make reference to "Snow-White and Rose-Red"?

Divine Secrets
of the Ya-Ya Sisterhood
(1996) BY REBECCA WELLS

Rory refers to the whole late-night Puffs initiation as a "Ya-Ya Sisterhood" thing, but this bestselling novel about a close but estranged mother and daughter feels like one whose lessons could be applied to many other mother-daughter pairs in this series. Do you think the characters of Vivi and Sidda are more like Lorelai and Rory, Emily and Lorelai, or Mrs. Kim and Lane? Why do you think that?

To Kill a Mockingbird
(1960) BY HARPER LEE

Jess refers to Stars Hollow's town meetings, which Rory and Lorelai dutifully attend, as "so *To Kill a Mockingbird*." Why do you think Jess uses this reference in relation to Stars Hollow's town meetings? Have you ever attended town or community meetings? Do you find them exhilarating, like Lorelai and Rory do, or tedious, like Jess and Luke do?

Also, for the number of times Lorelai references Boo Radley, the novel's mysterious town recluse who, it turns out, is protective and kind, we'd have to assume she loves this story. Do you think she feels a certain affinity to Boo Radley, or simply thinks every town needs a Boo Radley, as she says in a season 3 town meeting?

The Catcher in the Rye
(1951) BY J. D. SALINGER

Rory calls Jess out for "trying to be Holden Caulfield," the angsty, rebellious teen in Salinger's *The Catcher in the Rye*. Holden spends the novel running from his problems; he fights a classmate who went on a date with a girl he liked; he disparages others as phonies and is extremely judgmental of everyone else's motives—it sounds like Rory's assessment was right on the nose. But what do you see as Holden's—and Jess's—good qualities? What has made Holden a relatable character to readers for seventy-plus years? And are those qualities among the same reasons Jess has been a fan-favorite for twenty-plus years?

Romeo and Juliet
(1597) BY WILLIAM SHAKESPEARE

When Rory, Paris, Tristan, and their group are given the final act of *Romeo and Juliet* to interpret and perform in any style they wish, Paris decrees that they will be going with a traditional Elizabethan theme. If you were given free rein to reimagine the famed death scene, what style or theme would you have chosen? And who would you cast in which roles?

Unfinished Business: Memoirs 1902–1988
(2000) BY JOHN HOUSEMAN

As part of their prep, Paris printed out the chapters on acting from Houseman's memoirs. The Romanian-born actor was famous for his collaborations with Orson Welles, his screenplays, his work as a theater producer, and his best supporting actor Oscar for 1973's *The Paper Chase*. Did you know who Houseman was before reading his memoir? If you were to read advice on acting, who would be your top five actors to seek out?

The Mourning Bride
(1697) BY WILLIAM CONGREVE

The oft-misquoted (and misattributed) phrase "Hell hath no fury like a woman scorned" comes from this tragic play about a king (unsuccessfully) trying to break up the marriage of his daughter to the son of his enemy. Be honest—did you know this line, as quoted by Louise, was *not* Shakespeare?

The Scarecrow of Oz
(1915) BY L. FRANK BAUM

Among the books that Rory has hidden away in her dresser drawer filing system, this book, the ninth of Baum's fourteen novels set in Oz (and allegedly Baum's personal favorite), was visible on top. Throughout the series, the Scarecrow becomes King of Emerald City, serves as an advisor to Princess Ozma, and helps overthrow King Krewl of Jinxland. Who was your favorite character in the Oz universe as a child, and did that change as you got older?

Contact
(1985) BY CARL SAGAN

Another book in Rory's dresser drawer is this science fiction classic, which was the astronomer and astrophysicist's only work of fiction. It also seems like a rarity in Rory's collection—we don't see or hear her talk about science fiction, heavy science, or books by scientists. Do you think her reading this novel was an attempt to cross into that genre?

A HISTORY DEEP DIVE
WITH RICHARD

———∞⨯∞———

While chatting about books with Rory, Richard mentions that he has "several" Winston Churchill biographies on his bookshelves. This seems apt, considering his affinity for multivolume histories and larger-than-life figures. Also, after his mother, Trix, moved to London, he and Emily would visit her yearly—he could have amassed quite the collection from shops around the Bulldog's old stomping grounds.

Richard doesn't mention which books on the revered British prime minister he has, but we imagine it would include Churchill's own six-volume history of World War II and that he'd certainly add newer releases to that shelf.

- *My Early Life* (1930) by Winston Churchill
- *The Second World War* (1948–1953) by Winston Churchill
  - *The Gathering Storm* (1948)
  - *Their Finest Hour* (1949)
  - *The Grand Alliance* (1950)
  - *The Hinge of Fate* (1950)
  - *Closing the Ring* (1951)
  - *Triumph and Tragedy* (1953)
- *Churchill: A Life* (1991) by Martin Gilbert

- *In Command of History: Churchill Fighting and Writing the Second World War* (2005) by David Reynolds
- *Churchill: Walking with Destiny* (2018) by Andrew Roberts
- *Churchill: Wanted Dead or Alive* (2019) by Celia Sandys
- *Churchill, Master and Commander: Winston Churchill at War 1895–1945* (2021) by Anthony Tucker-Jones

The Fountainhead
(1943) BY AYN RAND

While Rory and Jess discuss literature, she recommends this novel about an uncompromising young architect who embodies the individualism Rand advocated for. Rory said she read this at age ten but didn't understand it, so had to give it another go at age fifteen (imagine your average fourth or fifth grader reading this seven-hundred-page tome, regardless of how great Rand's "forty-page monologues" are). Why do you think Jess hasn't been able to finish it yet? Was this book on your radar in high school?

The Children's Hour
(1934) BY LILLIAN HELLMAN

Rory buys this play at the bookstore for Lorelai, who had previously mentioned wanting to read it while they were watching *Julia*, a 1977 movie in which Jane Fonda plays the author Lillian Hellman. Hellman was a successful playwright and memoirist who was also blacklisted during the height of McCarthyism. This play, which was based on a nineteenth-century Scottish court case, involves a girl at a boarding school who falsely accuses the two headmistresses of having a lesbian relationship. One of the central struggles of the characters, however, is what is and isn't appropriate for fourteen-year-old girls to know or do, and whether or not the teachers should be treating them as children or adults. This is also something Lorelai seems to struggle with regarding Rory—when should she treat her as an adult, and when should she assert her authority as the parental figure? What do you think she would take away from the play? What do you think of her overall parenting style?

BONUS READ: The 1977 movie *Julia* that Rory and Lorelai watched was based on a "portrait" chapter of Hellman's book *Pentimento* (1973). The character of Julia is widely believed to be based heavily on the life of Muriel Gardiner, an American heiress and psychoanalyst who, while living in Vienna during the 1930s, smuggled hundreds of people out of the country and housed and funded Resistance members. Hellman denied the chapter was based on Gardiner, but the similarities between her piece and Gardiner's own 1983 memoir, *Code Name Mary*, are difficult to dispute. What do you think the true story is? And how enthralled do you think Lorelai might be about this real-life scandal?

Inherit the Wind
(1955) BY JEROME LAWRENCE AND ROBERT E. LEE

This play is a fictionalized account of the Scopes "Monkey" Trial, the highly publicized 1925 case of a high school teacher being sued by the state for teaching the theory of evolution. If Rory were to write a play based on a historical event, what story do you think she would choose? Would she fictionize it, or write it as true to fact as possible?

Letters to a Young Poet
(1929) BY RAINER MARIA RILKE

At the town book sale, Rory is happy to have found this in paperback (presumably for portability—she already owns it in hardback). In it, the real-life correspondence between Rilke and a teenage cadet at a military academy. The "young poet" in question, Franz Xaver Kappus, was weighing whether to pursue a life of letters or one in the military, and he wrote to Rilke asking for advice. Over the course of six years and ten letters, Rilke offered beautiful, timeless advice to trust your instincts, sit with your questions, and learn to live in the now. Do you think Rilke's letters are still relevant to artists today? Do you think a high-school Rory could have applied his advice to her own life and goals?

Like Water for Chocolate

(1989) BY LAURA ESQUIVEL

Kirk is also at the book sale, trying to haggle this romantic tragedy slash cookbook down a nickel at a time. In it, a woman, Tita, is not allowed to marry because of an old family tradition that the youngest daughter remain single in order to care for her aging mother. We never meet Kirk's mother on the show, but in the numerous references he makes of her, she sounds demanding and unconcerned about his feelings or well-being. He also lives with her well into adulthood and only considers moving out once he has a steady girlfriend. This is the only book we see Kirk with, besides two comic scenes where he's consulting *Hockey for Dummies* and *Yoga for Dummies*—do you think he spends so much time on new jobs and odd hobbies as a way to find an outlet to escape his mother, the way Tita had her cooking?

Franny and Zooey
(1961) BY J. D. SALINGER

Salinger packaged his short story, "Franny," with its companion novella, *Zooey*, for this release—Franny and Zooey are siblings in the Glass family that Salinger wrote about at least a half dozen times for the *New Yorker*. This is a book that both Rory and Jess have read, and when Lorelai catches Jess in Rory's room alone, he says he was looking to see if she had this book. Franny and Zooey enjoy discussing philosophy and are often seen comforting or helping the other through confusing times. If you have siblings, do you have that kind of relationship with them? Or, if you are an only child, like Jess and Rory were, did you seek out friends who could fill that role for you?

In Franny's story, she visits her boyfriend at Yale, and over the course of dinner, becomes increasingly disenchanted with him, his friends, and his braggadocio manner regarding a paper he wrote; at one point, she says, "I'm just so sick of pedants and conceited little tearer-downers I could scream . . . if I'd had any guts at all, I wouldn't have gone back to college at all this year." Do you see any parallels between Franny's story and Rory's future college years?

Frankenstein

(1818) BY MARY SHELLEY

As Jess eggs Dean on about how it's "just so darn cute" that he'd brought Rory some ice cream, he tells Dean his "Frankenstein scowl" really adds to his menacing towering-over-others act. Of course, it would be pedantic to point out that Dr. Frankenstein was the creator, and "the Creature" is the tall, scowling monster that he created. But the insult of calling someone a Frankenstein has come to mean that they are lumbering, dumb, and inherently bad, though that's not how Shelley wrote her Creature at all. Do you think Jess's taunt was fair or unnecessary? Do you think that Dean's image and reputation got "Frankensteined" during the course of the show? The boy we met in season 1 was confident, laid back, and intellectually curious—he would trade book recommendations with Rory and would read beyond his comfort zone at her behest. But once Jess came to town and Rory began to lose interest in him, Dean became close-minded, jealous, quick to anger, and presumably never reads again. Which boy were you rooting for on the show?

Memoirs of General W. T. Sherman

(1875) BY WILLIAM TECUMSEH SHERMAN

When Luke's uncle Louie dies, Luke goes out of his way to give the man the funeral he deserves—including buying an oversized casket to hold all the things Louie wanted to be buried with: fishing reel, bowling trophy, antique dueling pistols, thousands of baseball cards, a copy of Sherman's *Memoirs*. From what we know of Uncle Louie, he seems to be of similar temperament to the divisive Union general—gruff, pessimistic, irritable, headstrong. Do you know anyone who had a similarly long list of funerary requests? What would you like to be buried with?

Waiting for Godot
(1953) BY SAMUEL BECKETT

Lorelai references perhaps the most famous example of the Theatre of the Absurd during her own Friday Night Dinner of the Absurd. As the three Gilmore women sit around the table, Emily insists on not beginning the meal until Richard arrives. "It's been forever!" Lorelai claims. "Godot was just here—he said, 'I ain't waiting for Richard,' grabbed a roll, and left." Absurdism revolves around the idea that the universe has no meaning, and therefore searching for meaning is pointless and irrational—absurdism is essentially the opposite of existentialism. Absurdist theater has four main characteristics: absence, emptiness, nothingness, and unresolved mysteries. Do you think parts of *Gilmore Girls* fit this definition of absurdism? Who on the show most readily represents absurdism?

The Story of Doctor Dolittle
(1920) BY HUGH LOFTING

Michel calls Lorelai "a regular Dr. Dolittle" when she signs off on vaccinating some ducks in the pond at the Independence Inn. Considering all the jokes about

Lorelai's bad rap with animals—couldn't take care of a hamster, had a sick rabbit, somehow killed a turtle, lost Rory's class bird, etc.—Michel's sarcastic tone is even funnier. Why do you think Lorelai, who clearly loves animals, has such a bad track record with them? Do you know someone similar who, despite all their great qualities, just isn't a great pet owner, gardener, etc.?

Candide
(1759) BY VOLTAIRE

Rory mentions finishing this seminal French work that day, which is probably fair to assume was a class assignment. *Candide* is Voltaire's tragicomedy that rails against superfluous optimism and hope and the dogma of religion. The memorable adage at the end, when Candide and his friends choose to live on a farm, is "We must cultivate our own garden." What do you think that means? Do you read it as "we should all mind our own business," or "we should put our own needs first"? How might the meaning differ depending on the mood or circumstances of the reader?

The Bhagavad Gita
(1ST MILLENNIUM BCE)

"It's not the *Bhagavad Gita*!" Paris snaps at Madeline in frustration when she deemed her reading of a class outline too slow. She's referring to the seven-hundred-verse Hindu book of scripture, which covers themes like karma, a core philosophical tenet of Hinduism. *Karma* means "action," and the intent behind the action has an effect on its consequences. Do you think Paris believes in karma, either good or bad? When are the times when it seems she does or does not?

Please Kill Me: The Uncensored Oral History of Punk

(1996) BY LEGS McNEIL AND GILLIAN McCAIN

As Rory attempts to help Jess study the Marshall Plan, he wastes time doing magic tricks, prying into Dean's whereabouts, and asking if she's read *Please Kill Me* (she hasn't but admits she would like to borrow it). Compiled from hundreds of interviews with the most important people in punk rock including musicians, artists, managers, and promoters, its pages are full of all the dirty, intimate details that make you want to put on a ripped tee and leather jacket and hit Max's Kansas City (RIP) and CBGB (RIP, OMFUG). Do you enjoy reading oral histories, like this one, of various cultural movements or works that you're into? Do you think it's important to already know some of the voices in these pieces, or can someone with limited knowledge on the subject learn just as much through reading them? Why do you think that?

THE NEW YORK TIMES
DAILY CROSSWORD PUZZLES, VOLUME 36
(1994) by Eugene T. Maleska

Standing in line at Doose's, Lorelai flips through an over-sized puzzle book and says she hates crosswords because they make her feel stupid, "but if you don't do them, you're not only stupid, you're also a coward." This is actually an inside joke—Lauren Graham would often do crosswords while waiting on set, as would Kelly Bishop and Edward Herrmann (Emily and Richard). How often do you do crossword puzzles? And how often do you *finish* crossword puzzles?

Othello

(1603) BY WILLIAM SHAKESPEARE

Jess continues to derail his tutoring session with Rory and manages to convince her to go out for ice cream. She agrees on the stipulation that she'll read him *Othello* on the drive. *Othello* is a play driven by jealousy, primarily over Desdemona's love. As much as Jess has been needling at Dean with the aim of getting him and Rory to break up, do you think he was calculated in thinking how much more jealous Dean would become if he knew Jess had been in Rory's car—a gift that Dean worked incredibly hard on for her? If you had been in Rory's shoes, would you have let Jess drive the car?

The Little Locksmith
(1943) BY KATHARINE BUTLER HATHAWAY

To help cheer Rory up as she walks around on her first day with a wrist cast, Lorelai surprises her with *The Little Locksmith*, a posthumous memoir by a woman who spent a decade of her childhood strapped to a board to try to curb the effects of spinal tuberculosis. Despite her difficult childhood and lifelong deformity, Hathaway pursues independence, creativity, and responds to life's challenges in a way that would make the more modern body positivity movement proud. Rory clearly already knows this story, but how sweet is Lorelai's gift (even if it does fall into her special, patented, dark-humor kind of love language)?

"The Celebrated Jumping Frog of Calaveras County"
(1865) BY MARK TWAIN

In a funny aside about how they don't patronize the next town over, Lorelai jokingly justifies it because "didn't they feed lead to our jumping frog or something?" Spoiler alert: That's the entire plot of Twain's short story, but the broader symbolism of the piece is about how and why small communities often have an attitude of healthy distrust toward outsiders. In how many ways does Lorelai personify this inclination throughout the show? How do others within Stars Hollow?

"The Lottery"
(1948) BY SHIRLEY JACKSON

Speaking of small-town mentalities, Rory brings up Shirley Jackson's deeply upsetting "The Lottery"—when the *New Yorker* first published it in June 1948, they received more mail in response to it than they had for any other work of fiction. Some even canceled their subscriptions. For all of the intense reactions the short story caused (hint: this is one lottery you do not want to win), the work speaks to scapegoating and mob mentality and how that can take place even in idyllic settings. Is this characterization of small towns reflective of Stars Hollow? In what ways has its townspeople punished people in metaphorically similar ways? Have you ever felt this about any communities you've lived in?

What Color Is Your Parachute?

(2001 EDITION) BY RICHARD NELSON BOLLES

As Christopher tells Lorelai when she finds this among other things in her business-school graduation gift basket, this practical manual for job hunters will "help you answer two questions: what do you want to do and where do you want to do it?" This guide has been updated annually since 1970 and is a helpful source for not only searching for a job but also finding the type of career you will thrive in. Do you think managing the Independence Inn is a job that Lorelai is naturally suited for, or one that she stumbled into because of Mia's benevolence? If she weren't running an inn, what career could you see Lorelai succeeding in?

The Portable Nietzsche
(1954) BY FRIEDRICH NIETZSCHE

Another graduation gift basket find from Christopher—
"light, cheery reading," he claims. But of the four major
works included in this collection, Nietzsche's *Twilight of
the Idols* contains some well-known aphorisms ("What
does not destroy me makes me stronger") and other
pithy lines that she would enjoy. One of the other works
included, *The Anti-Christ* or *Nietzsche contra Wagner* (1889),
is Nietzsche's very personal attack on his once close
friend, the composer Richard Wagner. Do you think this
burn-book style of essay is essentially a more highbrow
version of the tawdry autobiographies Lorelai enjoys?
Do you like learning about feuds between historical
people? If our modern-day tabloids had existed back
then, what might the headlines have been regarding
Nietzsche and Wagner?

Rebecca of Sunnybrook Farm

(1903) BY KATE DOUGLAS WIGGIN

When Paris learns that her fellow students find her smart and competent but wouldn't vote for her for student body president because of her obviously dismal likability polling, she decides to convince Rory to be her running mate. "Rebecca of Sunnybrook Farm for the new millennium!" Paris proclaims. In the books, Rebecca is a sweet, imaginative girl who goes to live with her two aunts when her family's finances become dire. Do you think the other Chilton students view Rory as a Rebecca? Have you seen this type of pairing tactic in other voting scenarios, whether school or political? Do you think it works?

SEASON 3

Wherein Rory is in her senior year at Chilton; after months of tension because of Rory's obvious feelings for Jess, Dean very publicly dumps her; Rory starts dating Jess; Rory is accepted to Harvard, Yale, and Princeton, and ultimately chooses Yale; the Independence Inn is damaged in a fire; Lorelai and Sookie buy the Dragonfly Inn; Lane starts her band, Hep Alien, and tries to date the guitarist, Dave Rygalski; Jess hops a bus for California without telling anyone, including Rory; Rory graduates as valedictorian.

A Bolt from the Blue and Other Essays

(2002) BY MARY McCARTHY

Besides being a successful novelist, McCarthy was also a literary and social critic and essayist who was published on topics ranging from fashion magazines to Watergate. Do you think Rory enjoys essay collections like these or novels more? When a writer, such as McCarthy, does both, which do you think gives the reader a better sense of their talents?

The Bell Jar
(1963) BY SYLVIA PLATH

While discussing who Rory should write her college entrance essay on, Lorelai suggests picking a favorite author, like perhaps Faulkner. Rory immediately suggests Sylvia Plath, and Lorelai questions if that choice could send the wrong message, because of the "whole head in the oven thing." For all of Plath's emotive, despairing (and often darkly funny) writing, she has nonetheless become an ongoing cultural punch line for suicide. Do you think Plath is a good topic for a "person you admire" essay? What author would you (or did you) pick for this type of essay in high school? Would you change your answer now?

POP QUIZ!

Rory and Lorelai have lunch with the Springsteens, a family whose father, Darren, is an influential Harvard alum and who has two perky, preppy children primed for the Harvard track. During the meal, Darren begins a friendly game of quizzing the table, and his children readily play along.

Q: Where did the phrase "one fell swoop" come from?

A: Coined in *Macbeth* and derived from Middle English.

Q: In which play does Falstaff appear?

A: *Henry IV* and *The Merry Wives of Windsor*. (Note that while Darren also brings up *Henry V* as a Falstaff play, the comedic favorite was only eulogized in that play—he dies offstage and another character describes his death, but no actor playing Falstaff appears.)

Rory pops in with a win when she correctly identifies the mythological figure with the head of a man, the body of a lion, and the tail of a scorpion, which was also the title of a Robertson Davies novel. The whole table is impressed when she chimes in with *The Manticore*.

- *Macbeth* (c. 1606) by William Shakespeare
- *Henry IV* parts 1 and 2 (c. 1597) by William Shakespeare
- *The Merry Wives of Windsor* (1602) by William Shakespeare
- *Henry V* (1599) by William Shakespeare
- *The Manticore* (1972) by Robertson Davies

Does your family ever play quiz games, either on-the-spot like the Springsteens or via a deck of Trivial Pursuit cards or some other premade quiz set? Which are your favorite categories for these games?

Norton Critical Edition Reference Books

After Lorelai tells a bad joke and Rory informs her "how about that schnitzel!" is a terrible punch line, Lorelai chides her that no one asked for the Norton Critical Edition. This popular hundred-year-old brand of annotated publications provides helpful footnotes and historical and cultural context to a wide variety of classic and modern literature—including a large number of the books mentioned in these pages. And while Norton hadn't published any joke compilations or musings on comedy at the time this episode aired, they did publish one a few years later where Lorelai could have found a better punch line: Jim Holt's *Stop Me If You've Heard This: A History and Philosophy of Jokes*.

Letters of Ayn Rand
(1995) EDITED BY MICHAEL S. BERLINER

Rory makes a habit of reading collections of the letters and journals of authors she loves. We've seen her do it with Dawn Powell and Sylvia Plath, and here again with Ayn Rand. For books like this, which cover a wide variety of letters, are you a completist who reads start to finish in its entirety, or do you skip around based on theme or era?

A Christmas Carol
(1843) BY CHARLES DICKENS

It might not have been Christmas during the annual Stars Hollow dance marathon, but anytime Taylor Doose comes around, Luke's inner Scrooge rears its irritated head. "You would kick Tiny Tim's crutch out from under him, wouldn't you?" Taylor said, exasperated that Luke refused his request to donate coffee to serve the contestants and audience. "If he asked for a free cup of coffee, gimpy's going down," Luke retorted. Why do you think Luke, who is incredibly generous to many people in their community, is so opposed to contributing to town events?

The Art of War
(5TH CENTURY BCE) BY SUN TZU

"You want to play rough, fine," Rory says as she circles Francie in the restroom, trying to outwit the bully. "I read *The Art of War*." Rory and everyone else! This 2,500-year-old text—which covers everything from calculating existing factors, planning an attack, understanding strengths and weaknesses, dealing with contingencies, espionage, and how to avoid battles all together—has been cited by everyone from actual war generals like Douglas MacArthur to the NFL's Super Bowl–winningest coach Bill Belichick to philosophic rappers like Tupac Shakur. (And numerous fictional characters too, from Tony Soprano to Commander Riker and Captain Picard.) Do you think Rory's reading of this timeless strategy book helped her at all in her ongoing battles with Francie and Paris? Or in any of her maneuvering with her mother or grandparents? How much of *The Art of War* do you think can actually be applied to a regular person's life or workplace?

Eloise: A Book for Precocious Grown-ups
(1955) BY KAY THOMPSON

As high school graduation nears, Paris is reading through guest commencement speaker suggestions submitted by the students, and she can't tell which are real and which are pranks. Princess Diana's butler? Dr. Phil? "Watch Choate get Joan Didion while we're being read *Eloise at the Plaza*," she scoffs. Set in New York's Plaza Hotel, Eloise is a mischievous six-year-old who lives in the penthouse with her nanny and pet pug and turtle and wreaks havoc throughout the hotel. The book was a bestseller, and it inspired the Plaza to create an actual Eloise suite and host daily Eloise teas. If Rory had been closer to her grandparents when she was in elementary school, do you think Emily would have approved or disapproved of the Eloise-themed tea? What about Lorelai? Would you have loved an Eloise tea at that age?

The Great Gatsby
(1925) BY F. SCOTT FITZGERALD

When Sookie runs into an old culinary school friend who makes it clear he still has feelings for her, Lorelai reacts by telling her his ten-year crush is "some serious *Great Gatsby* pining—you're his Daisy." Have you harbored unrequited feelings for someone for that long? Or seen it happen to people you know? Would you go to the lengths Jay Gatsby did—amassing a fortune through criminal dealings, or some other more relevant grand gesture—in order to win that person's love or attention?

Julius Caesar
(c. 1599) BY WILLIAM SHAKESPEARE

Just like everyone knows a Benedict Arnold is a traitor, calling someone a Brutus means they've betrayed you. As it turns out, Francie outplayed Rory, and Paris feels that Rory has figuratively stabbed her in the back. And though Rory knows Francie set her up, she did slip up and mention Paris's secret boyfriend, when she'd promised Paris she wouldn't. Similarly to Rory, Brutus prides himself on his ethical code and his honor, but he is also naïve in how his actions would be perceived and overthinks every decision to the point of madness. Do you think Rory can see a bit of herself in his complex character? And could Paris see how she often acts as a Brutus, or does she have too much main-character energy to see herself in that role?

The Diary of Virginia Woolf

[5 VOLUMES] (1977–1984)
EDITED BY ANNE OLIVIER BELL

This five-volume set of Virginia Woolf's diaries seems to be Rory's latest lunchtime reading material (based on the color of the cover, she appears to be in the middle of Volume 4, covering 1931–1935). Woolf kept her diaries around to revisit them, and she salvaged many from her London home after it was bombed in October 1940. What would you try to save from your home if you were in that situation? Diaries, photo albums, heirlooms?

EURO TRIP!

———◇◇◇◇◇◇———

Lorelai and Rory excitedly start planning their European vacation—they've long talked about backpacking through all the major cities once Rory graduates high school, which Richard and Emily find absolutely ludicrous. Backpacking and staying in hostels? Who would *do* such a thing?!

Of course, considering the luxury hotels and services Richard and Emily require when traveling, they can't imagine themselves or their family members doing something so grand while sticking to a budget. (Fun fact: It's completely possible to visit the Vatican and the Uffizi without a private tour guide! Thousands of people do it each year!) However, even though these particular guides that Lorelai and Rory are consulting are now a couple of decades out of date, Rick Steves, the popular travel writer who encourages travelers to visit less touristy locations in addition to the staples, continues to update his numerous guides, and countless other budget-friendly guides are available for vacationers who still have bills to pay back home. (And no, no budget guides encourage people "to sleep in a park like a squirrel," to quote Emily.)

And, if you do happen to have some extra cash to burn, plenty of guides for high-end travel are also available, even if the three Emily sent to Lorelai are woefully out of date.

- *Europe Through the Back Door* (2003) by Rick Steves
- *The Rough Guide to Europe on a Budget* (2003) by Rough Guides
- *Selected Hotels of Europe* (1987) by Fodor's
- *Hotels, Restaurants and Inns of Great Britain and Ireland* (1986) by Egon Ronay
- *Myra Waldo's Travel and Motoring Guide to Europe* (1978) by Myra Waldo

The Divine Comedy
(1321) BY DANTE ALIGHIERI

This epic narrative poem, which we see Jess reading and which Rory has previously referenced, is widely considered to be one of the most important masterworks of world literature. In it, Dante's journey to the divine takes him through the three parts of death that make up the complete *Comedy*: *Inferno* (hell), *Purgatorio* (purgatory), and *Paradiso* (heaven). Dante wove in numerous biblical ideas while also making his work a political satire, which included mentioning which of the nine rings of hell various popes and political leaders would end up in. If Rory were to recast the parts with more modern references, which of her favorite writers, leaders, and musicians would end up where? What about your personal recasting?

The Holy Barbarians
(1959) BY LAWRENCE LIPTON

Rory's excitement as she shows off her latest find to Jess is palpable, and it's sweet how receptive he is and how well their taste in books align.

"*The Holy Barbarians*. I mean, what a title. And it's by a Venice Beach beatnik about Venice Beach beatniks, and to top it off, the beatnik who wrote it is the father of the guy that does those Actors Studio interviews on TV."

Presuming Rory finished this off relatively quickly and then did let Jess borrow it, as she promised to, do you think it might have had any influence on his sudden decision to hop a bus and head out to . . . Venice Beach?

Encyclopedia Brown: Boy Detective
(1963) BY DONALD J. SOBOL

Jess mocks Luke by saying if a book in his collection "doesn't have Encyclopedia Brown in the title, that narrows it down a lot," but the joke's on him—this classic kid's series is fun. Be honest—how many of Leroy Brown's neighborhood mysteries could you solve before turning to the answers page in the back?

Speaking of Luke's bookshelves, a handful of titles that can be seen during the series include:

- *Forty Days* (1992) by Bob Simon, a memoir by the news correspondent about his time being held hostage in an Iraqi prison during the Gulf War.
- *Fatal Terrain* (1997) by Dale Brown, a wartime techno-thriller.
- *Hotel Berlin '43* (1944) by Vicki Baum, a novel set in a luxury hotel during the last days of WWII.

Not exactly Jess's taste, but also not at all an indicator of the dumbed-down version of his uncle that Jess seems to have.

> VOCAB: *Techno-thriller.* A hybrid genre in which much of the plot depends upon technical descriptions of computers, weapons, software, vehicles, or other machines, or the inner workings of certain disciplines, like espionage, military maneuvers, or martial arts.

Lord Jim
(1900) BY JOSEPH CONRAD

Emily, upset that Jess showed up for dinner late, with a black eye, and in a horrible, surly mood, complains to Lorelai that he shouldn't be allowed to be around Rory, period. "I wanted to slap that monosyllabic mouth of his," Emily declared over the phone. "And God forbid they're in another accident together or his heap of a car breaks down and Lord Jim has decided cell phones are beneath him and they're stranded in the middle of nowhere." Lord Jim is the protagonist in Conrad's novel about a sailor who lives with the guilt that he abandoned a sinking ship without properly aiding its passengers. Though the book is primarily about Jim attempting to run from his shame, he does manage to get into a fistfight and then settles in an extremely remote village, away from anyone who might have known of his disgrace. Presumably Emily put fistfight and didn't-call-to-say-he'd-be-late-to-dinner together and got Lord Jim, even if the storylines don't exactly line up. If you were in Emily's shoes, who might make a better literary reference to express disapproval at Jess? And you can't say Holden Caulfield.

WORDS OF ADVICE

As Chilton prepares to celebrate its bicentennial, the students are given the chance to write speeches and compete for the honor of speaking to the gathered alumni and faculty and have their speech broadcast on C-SPAN. Of course, Headmaster Charleston changes the rules and decides to have Rory and Paris combine their speeches and present together. As they're currently fighting, neither is pleased. And once Paris finds out she wasn't accepted to Harvard, she tanks the entire speech, which Rory attempts to salvage by reciting their selected opening quotes about education and expanding one's mind.

- *Iacocca: An Autobiography* (1984) by Lee Iacocca with William Novak
  "Apply yourself. Get all the education you can, but then do something. Don't just stand there, make it happen."

- *Intentions* (1891) by Oscar Wilde
  "Education is an admirable thing, but it is well to remember from time to time that nothing that is worth knowing can be taught."

A third quote by Malcolm Forbes, the publisher of *Forbes* magazine and a former New Jersey state senator, was also used: "The purpose of education is to replace an empty mind with an open one."

Do you find any quotes particularly inspirational? While reading, do you pull out phrases or passages to save for future reference? Who are your go-to sources for inspiration?

WHEN IT RAINS, IT POES

———◇◇◇◇◇———

The Edgar Allan Poe Society visits Stars Hollow, and that means countless mustachioed men reciting "The Raven," and Lorelai dropping as many references around the guests at the inn as she can. Did they land? Not a bit. Did the town enjoy the society's little convention? Nevermore.

- "The Raven" (1845) by Edgar Allan Poe
- "The Tell-Tale Heart" (1843) by Edgar Allan Poe
- "The Cask of Amontillado" (1846) by Edgar Allan Poe
- "The System of Doctor Tarr and Professor Fether" (1845) by Edgar Allan Poe

Why do you think Stars Hollow as a whole disliked the very quirky, themed Poe Society events when, historically, they love quirky, themed events? Is his writing simply too dark and dreary for their idyllic little town?

In Search of Lost Time
(1927) BY MARCEL PROUST

While Paris is hiding out in bed after not getting into Harvard, she tries to justify staying there with "Proust wrote all three thousand pages of *In Search of Lost Time* in bed; if it's good enough for him . . ." Granted, Proust was always in poor health and spent much of his adult life effectively bedridden, but many other creatives have also chosen to work from the comfort of their feather beds and down pillows. Mark Twain, Edith Wharton, and William Wordsworth were all known to write longhand in their beds, and Truman Capote told the *Paris Review:* "I am a completely horizontal author; I can't think unless I'm lying down." Do you like working or reading in bed? Do you find the comfort of a bed conducive to thinking and writing, or is it too laid-back and relaxing to stay in a productive frame of mind?

VOCAB: *Librocubicularist.* Someone who reads in bed.

Nicholas Nickleby
(1839) BY CHARLES DICKENS

Lorelai was exaggerating just a bit when she referred to Rory's college choice pro/con list as being a "document the length of *Nicholas Nickleby*," as this stereotypically Dickensian tome clocks in at around nine hundred fifty pages, but Rory is known for extensive pro/conning, so who knows. *Nicholas Nickleby* does have a protracted plot revolving around a corrupt boarding school for children, though one which the children had no choice about attending. Were you surprised when Rory chose Yale over Harvard? Do you think she made the right choice? If given the choice between any top universities, which would you choose, and why?

MRS. KIM GIVETH
AND MRS. KIM TAKETH AWAY

———◦◇◇◇◦———

Lane screwed up. After months of running around starting a band and trying to slyly date Dave Rygalski, the cute, music-nerd guitarist who has played along with Lane's crazy schemes to hide her life from her mom (remember when he pretended to be a Christian guitarist, and played the Kim family Thanksgiving incognito?), Lane got drunk and spilled all the beans to her mom. Dave comes over to course-correct. He presents himself and his long list of good-boy qualifications to Mrs. Kim and asks if he can take Lane to prom; she cryptically replies, "Let never day nor night unhallowed pass, but still remember what the Lord hath done."

Dave and Lane presume it's from the Bible, so Dave stays up all night reading it cover to cover. When he comes back exhausted and defeated, Mrs. Kim informs him it's not from the Bible—it's Shakespeare.

- *Henry VI* (c. 1592) by William Shakespeare
- The Bible (c. 1450s)

That particular line from *Henry VI* is spoken by the king after he meets a man who claims to have had his blindness cured. Do you think Mrs. Kim was saying this as a way to tell Dave she's thankful he sees Lane for who she is? Or that she herself now sees them both, and is trying to adjust her means of parenting? Or was she truly just "goofing off," as she told Dave?

Eleanor Roosevelt: Volume 1, 1884–1933

(1992) BY BLANCHE WIESEN COOK

The first of an eventual three-volume set, this award-winning biography of America's longest-serving first lady covered the first forty years of her life, up through her time as First Lady of New York. The second volume, *The Defining Years, 1933–1938*, came out in 2000, so presumably Rory was reading the then-decade-old first volume so that she could move along to the next. (A third and final volume, *The War Years and After, 1939–1962*, was released in 2016.) Do you think Rory sees parts of herself in Roosevelt?

One of Roosevelt's most famous quotes is: "No one can make you feel inferior without your consent." Considering this was the book Rory was reading on the bus when she saw Jess for the last time before he disappeared to California, do you think that was foreshadowing her feelings at all? Do you think she and Jess brought out the best or worst in each other, or somewhere in the gray area?

The Lovely Bones
(2002) BY ALICE SEBOLD

When Emily told Lorelai she'd read this for her book club, Lorelai was immediately suspicious—one, because her mother was being cagey; and two, because this dark novel about a teen girl's murder and the subsequent years when her spirit watches her family try to solve the mystery of her disappearance and deal with the fallout of their grief is not exactly the kind of book you'd expect to see Emily reading. Somehow, Emily's on-the-spot review—"it's not my taste, but I respect the attempt"—was funny enough to overlook how tragic the book in question was. Have you ever been in a book club that chose something you'd describe as "not my taste, but I respect the attempt"? If you get partway through a book club selection and decide you don't like it, do you finish for the sake of participation and completism, or do you boldly fess up to not having finished the chosen work?

RORY GRADUATES, AND DELIVERS QUITE THE VALEDICTORIAN SPEECH

—◇◇◇◇◇—

After three long, hard years at Chilton, Rory is set to graduate at the top of the Class of 2003. In typical Rory style, she writes a lovely, moving commencement speech about the people and places—both real and fictional—that have shaped her life thus far.

> *I live in two worlds. One is a world of books.*
> *I've been a resident of Faulkner's Yoknapatawpha County,*
> *hunted the white whale aboard the* Pequod, *fought along-*
> *side Napoleon, sailed a raft with Huck and Jim, committed*
> *absurdities with Ignatius J. Reilly, rode a sad train with*
> *Anna Karenina and strolled down Swann's Way.*

"I've been a resident of Faulkner's Yoknapatawpha County"
Faulkner set fourteen novels and more than fifty stories in his fictional county of Yoknapatawpha, Mississippi. It was inspired by the real Lafayette County in northern Mississippi, where Faulkner lived most of his life. Presumably, Rory had spent more time in what Faulkner called his "apocryphal county" than just reading the aforementioned *The Sound and the Fury*.

Other trips to Yoknapatawpha County can be found in:

- *Sartoris* (1929)
- *As I Lay Dying* (1930)
- *Sanctuary* (1931)
- *Light in August* (1932)
- *Absalom, Absalom!* (1936)
- *The Unvanquished* (1938)
- *The Hamlet* (1940)
- *Go Down, Moses* (1942)
- *Intruder in the Dust* (1948)
- *Requiem for a Nun* (1951)
- *The Town* (1957)
- *The Mansion* (1959)
- *The Reivers* (1962)
- *Flags in the Dust* (1973)

"Hunted the white whale aboard the *Pequod*"

Melville's *Moby-Dick*

"Fought alongside Napoleon" Tolstoy's *War and Peace*

"Sailed a raft with Huck and Jim"

Twain's *The Adventures of Huckleberry Finn*

"Committed absurdities with Ignatius J. Reilly"

Toole's *A Confederacy of Dunces*

"Rode a sad train with Anna Karenina"

Tolstoy's *Anna Karenina*

"Strolled down Swann's Way" *Swann's Way*, the first volume of Proust's *In Search of Lost Time*

You may have noticed a trend here. All of these great, noble classics were written by . . . white men. Granted, many of these authors—notably Faulkner, Twain, and Toole—addressed slavery and racial prejudice in America by prominently featuring Black characters, but this list of literary places she's visited feels very much like the curated, of-the-era list of a turn-of-the-twenty-first-century New England prep school.

Contrast that with the role models she says her mother filled their home with: Jane Austen, Eudora Welty, Patti Smith. Though it's unclear which Austen or Smith books Rory has read (there's a reason Patti Smith is called the "punk poet laureate"—she's also won a National Book Award!), it's reassuring that she mentioned a handful of female influences as well.

Were you surprised by the list that Rory recited in her commencement speech? We've heard her wax poetic about authors like Dawn Powell and Sylvia Plath—would either of those choices have felt more surprising to someone in the audience? If you were writing a similar list of favorite books when you were graduating high school, what would you have included?

To see a list of more broadly inclusive books, especially curated with Rory's tastes in mind, check out page 221 for "Keep Reading with Rory," a post–*Gilmore Girls* reading challenge.

JESS'S ESSENTIAL READS

Of Rory's primary paramours, none matched her passion for reading quite like brooding bookworm Jess Mariano. Mirroring Jess's own contempt for societal pressures, disdain for authority, and general angsty rebelliousness, his reading choices trended heavily toward Beat Generation poets, gonzo journalism, and authors who understood loners and outsiders.

On the Road (1957) by Jack Kerouac
(season 2, episode 5)

On the Road is widely considered the most important novel of the Beat Generation, even though it is often criticized for seemingly glorifying young men for leading irresponsible lives. Do you think Jess related more to the characters' pursuit of existential meaning, or their literal freedom while he's stuck in Stars Hollow?

Do you think Jess reading this book (in which the characters road-trip from the East Coast out to California) foreshadowed his own journey west, or was more to signal his own deep love of reading?

Fear and Loathing in Las Vegas (1971)
by Hunter S. Thompson (season 2, episode 5)

We see Jess reading this book, and Thompson is an author Dean once recommended to Rory—it's one of the few ways those two characters ever overlapped, literarily. The innovator of gonzo journalism, Hunter S. Thompson put himself (or in this case, a thinly veiled version of himself) right in the center of any story he told, even when that story was taking so many hallucinogens that he couldn't understand or complete the assignments he was in Vegas for in the first place. How reliable a narrator do you think Raoul Duke (Thompson's nom de plume) is? How might the entire work be different if he had been sober throughout? Do you think this book is fitting for both Jess and Dean, or just one of them? Why?

Notes of a Dirty Old Man (1969)
by Charles Bukowski (season 2, episode 15)

Much like the collections of essays and columns that Rory likes to read, *Notes of a Dirty Old Man* is a selection of just over a year's worth of Bukowski's columns for his friend's underground L.A. newspaper. The stories are comical and irreverent, and it's easy to see the cigarette hanging out of Buk's mouth and the beers piled around his desk as he typed up these absurd stories. Do you enjoy these kinds of no-holds-barred confessions of drunken debauchery? Do you find it entertaining or not, and can you imagine essays like this being published in your local indie newspaper (or email newsletter) today? On a scale of one to ten, how many bemused Jess smirks do you rate it?

Slaughterhouse-Five (1969) by Kurt Vonnegut (season 2, episode 19)

Every nihilistic teenager goes through a Vonnegut phase, and this semiautobiographical antiwar novel is among his best. Oft-banned and once called "depraved, immoral, psychotic, vulgar, and anti-Christian" by a ruling judge, it's also an important work that shows the realistic and devastating effects of war on soldiers and the cities destroyed. Jess was reading this in the months following September 11, 2001, which, notably, was not discussed or even alluded to on the show except for a quick "post-9/11 environment" quip when Rory is moving into college in season 4. How do you think Vonnegut—who enlisted in 1942 after dropping out of college, was taken as a POW following the Battle of the Bulge, and narrowly survived the firebombing of Dresden—would have reacted if he were Jess's age in 2001? Does this famously antiwar book read differently to you by knowing Vonnegut's own experiences with war?

Vonnegut published *SH5* against the backdrop of fierce dissent and protests by young Americans of the ongoing Vietnam War—did you or anyone you know participate in these or other antiwar protests? How did you and the people you knew react to the United States' actions post-9/11? What books and music did you find yourself consuming during that time?

The Electric Kool-Aid Acid Test (1968) by Tom Wolfe (season 2, episode 21)

After Jess skipped town, Rory finds him in NYC's Washington Square Park reading this book. It combines many of Jess's interests—written in a pre-gonzo New Journalism style, it follows real-life countercultural icon and LSD proponent Ken Kesey as he hits the road with his band, interacts with many of the Beat greats (Ginsberg and various Kerouac associates), and generally snubs his nose at the conventions of polite society. Would you ever try (or have you ever tried) hallucinogens? Why or why not?

Kesey and his Merry Pranksters were similar to, but distinctly different from, the Beat Generation. Which group, if either, do you more closely identify with, and why?

High Fidelity (1995) by Nick Hornby (season 2, episode 21)

Hornby once said he'd heard his work called a "comedy of depression," which he appreciated, since many of his characters fit that mold. Rob, the protagonist of *High Fidelity*, has very low self-confidence and is depressed about his latest girlfriend dumping him for a neighbor, so he goes out of his way to connect with other exes to find out why they rejected him. Both the book and its setting (Rob runs a record store, and he and his friends are constantly making mixtape-related lists and discussing music choices) feel like solid Jess vibes, so when he tells Rory he wants to take her to a New York record store "right out of *High Fidelity*," it feels like he's really letting her into his world. Have you ever felt as insecure as Rob about current or past relationships? In the spirit of *High Fidelity*'s famous lists, what are your top five deal-breakers in a relationship? The top five swoon-worthy things a paramour has done for you?

A Confederacy of Dunces (1980) by John Kennedy Toole (season 3, episode 2)

Ignatius J. Reilly, the protagonist of this posthumously published novel, is a lazy, egotistical blowhard who believes he's anachronistic and that some higher power is to blame for his shortcomings. Jess, who is hunched over this book behind the counter at Luke's while the diner is full of patrons, is currently dating (or, at least, publicly making out with) a girl whom Rory considers to be a dunce. Have you ever felt morally or intellectually superior to others, the way Reilly constantly does? Did you, or someone you know with similar proclivities, take those feelings to an extreme, the way Reilly does? How did others perceive you or that person afterward?

We Owe You Nothing—Punk Planet:
The Collected Interviews (2001) edited
by Daniel Sinker (season 3, episode 4)
The Chicago-based zine *Punk Planet* was more than just a music mag—it covered the entirety of punk subculture, including art, politics, labor movements, etc. This collection of interviews includes trailblazers like Sonic Youth's Thurston Moore, Sleater-Kinney, and a lede to an article that Jess certainly would have skipped ahead to: "Noam Chomsky is . . . probably the only professor at MIT to have been featured on records with the likes of Jello Biafra, Bad Religion, and Chumbawamba. He sure doesn't look the part . . . behind the wavy white hair and grandfatherly smile lurks a dangerous threat to the status quo." Which interviews in this book do you think Jess enjoyed the most? And how many of the bands' tees did he already own? Which of these bands speak to you the most?

Visions of Cody (1972)
by Jack Kerouac (season 3, episode 5)
An unofficial sequel to *On the Road*, this even-more-stream-of-consciousness story was published three years after Kerouac's death. Have you ever, like Jess, had the

overwhelming urge to hop in a car or bus and hit the road? Why or why not?

The Magic Mountain (1924)
by Thomas Mann (season 3, episode 7)

At Stars Hollow's twenty-four-hour danceathon, Jess, who refuses to participate, sits in the bleachers for hours reading this book and quietly antagonizing Rory and Dean. The protagonist, Castorp, in Mann's pre–Great War setting travels to Davos, Switzerland, to visit a cousin who is treating his tuberculous in a sanitorium high in the Alps. When Castorp too is diagnosed, he spends the next seven years meeting all manner of people who also come to take the mountain air for relief, and they educate him on life and the world far more than anyone in his life previously had. Do you see any parallels between Jess and Castorp—two young men who found themselves stuck in a situation far beyond their control? Have you ever had this feeling? Do you think it is easier/healthier to resist or embrace unasked-for events like this?

One Hundred Years of Solitude (1967) by
Gabriel García Márquez (season 3, episode 20)

Jess was on a bus, sneaking away to California when we see him reading García Márquez's masterpiece of magical realism, which tells the tale of seven generations of a family who establish their own town in the remote jungles of Colombia. Of the many types of solitude that exist within the book—solitude of power, pride, love, grief, death—which resonates with you the most? As much of the novel focuses on failures in parenting, do you see bits of your own life within these characters? Do you see parallels between the book's many parents, who often learn nothing from their mistakes, with those of Jess's mother Liz, whom Jess and Luke have both painted as a narcissistic, absentee parent?

Naked Lunch (1959) by William S. Burroughs (season 3, episode 21)

We may only see Jess browse this title at a bookstore, but there's no doubt he doubled back for it later on. The non-linear collection of vignettes follows Burroughs's alter ego, Lee, as he travels around looking for his next hit, and the haphazard structure of the novel has been (reverently) said to inspire "nightmares of literary anarchy." Jess seems fond of books that jump around and don't offer a clean, precise plotline. Do you like this kind of storytelling? Why or why not?

FUN FACT: Songwriters and college buds Walter Becker and Donald Fagen were both big Beats and

Burroughs fans. When they decided to start a band in 1971, they named it after a "revolutionary" steam-powered dildo from *Naked Lunch*: Steely Dan (a band Lorelai once banned the inn's harpist from playing).

Billy Budd and Other Tales (1924)
by Herman Melville (season 4, episode 12)

Left unfinished and then published some thirty-plus years after Melville's death, *Billy Budd* is a novella about a popular, handsome young sailor who is done in by both the envy of one enemy and the captain's strict adherence to martial law. It seems Jess would relate to feeling unjustly persecuted, but why else might he enjoy this story? Do you agree with the ending of the book? Do you agree with Jess's story arc and where/how he ends up?

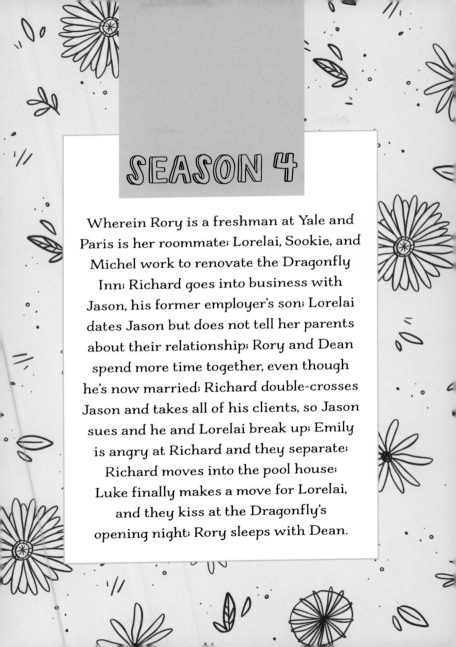

SEASON 4

Wherein Rory is a freshman at Yale and Paris is her roommate; Lorelai, Sookie, and Michel work to renovate the Dragonfly Inn; Richard goes into business with Jason, his former employer's son; Lorelai dates Jason but does not tell her parents about their relationship; Rory and Dean spend more time together, even though he's now married; Richard double-crosses Jason and takes all of his clients, so Jason sues and he and Lorelai break up; Emily is angry at Richard and they separate; Richard moves into the pool house; Luke finally makes a move for Lorelai, and they kiss at the Dragonfly's opening night; Rory sleeps with Dean.

Haiku,
Volume 2: Spring
(1981) BY R. H. BLYTH

On Rory's first day of class at Yale, she stuffs this book in her messenger bag. Reginald Horace Blyth was an English writer and professor who spent most of his adult life living in Korea and Japan. He studied under Zen masters and became a proponent of introducing Zen to western cultures, writing books on Zen and poetry, particularly haikus. Have you ever sat and studied Zen, or tried to apply its principles to your everyday life? Do you find Blyth's poetry to be a good entry point into Asian philosophies, as his contemporaries did?

Atonement
(2001) BY IAN McEWAN

This novel, which Rory was reading while waiting for classes to begin, is a study on perspective and lost innocence, and how one character can change the course of another's life by misreading what they see. College is often thought of as a time when students philosophize on their own beliefs and begin to better understand their own perspectives on life, in much the way that McEwan's characters do over the course of the novel. If you went to college, was there some fundamental belief that you changed or developed while there? Was it markedly different than what you thought before enrolling? Why do you think that is, or isn't?

Northanger Abbey
(1817) BY JANE AUSTEN

Published posthumously, *Northanger Abbey* has been called Austen's Gothic parody. Gothic stories feature three key motifs—a tense environment of fear, the haunting of the past on the present, and the supernatural—none of which Austen is known for. But *Northanger Abbey*'s heroine, Catherine, is intrigued by all things Gothic and imagines situations to be darker and more sinister than they truly are. Rory was reading this in the Stars Hollow gazebo when she discovers she's accidently come home on the weekend Dean and Lindsey are getting married. She was clearly opposed to their wedding, ostensibly because of their age but more likely because of her unresolved feelings for Dean. Have you or someone you know gotten married straight out of high school? Were you supportive or not? If Jane Austen were writing this storyline, how would she categorize Rory, Dean, and Lindsey?

The Sun Also Rises
(1926) BY ERNEST HEMINGWAY

We get a glimpse of Rory's literature class as one student asserts, "It's obvious that Hemingway is using Jake's impotence to indict a society which exploited its underclass to fight in the trenches of the First World War," to which Rory counters "Isn't Jake's impotence more about that generation's loss of faith and love?" While Rory's summation is the more typical reading of this Lost Generation *roman à clef*, might both readings be true? What do you think Jake's impotence—which was caused by a wartime groin injury—signifies? Do you think Hemingway's allegories about war are still relevant today?

Tender Is the Night
(1934) BY F. SCOTT FITZGERALD

Fitzgerald wrote this last novel about a young psychiatrist and his wife, who was one of his first patients, and the way her mental illness and his alcoholism doomed their marriage. Another prime example of a *roman à clef*, it covers many real-life Fitzgerald family issues, including their time in Europe seeking treatment for Zelda Fitzgerald's mental illness and the affairs each of them had. Do you think it makes a novel more or less interesting to discover it was based on real-life people or events? If you were to fictionalize a story from your life to write a novel, what names would you use for each of the characters?

> **VOCAB:** *Roman à clef.* French for "novel with a key," a *roman à clef* is a novel in which real people or events are thinly disguised with fictitious names. *On the Road*, *The Bell Jar*, and *Valley of the Dolls* are other notable examples of this.

"The Snows of Kilimanjaro"

(1936) BY ERNEST HEMINGWAY

Hemingway explores both the ever-presence of physical death and the death of a career and all the ways potential can be wasted through the dreams and memories of Harry, the story's protagonist. For a person having a midlife or end-of-life crisis, Harry's plight may feel profound or pertinent, but for college students who are just beginning to discover their paths, what do you think the primary takeaways would be?

Nineteen Eighty-Four
(1949) BY GEORGE ORWELL

Lorelai tells distraught, overdue Sookie, who is attempting to induce labor by bouncing around for two hours straight, that she wants to show her something from 1984. "The book?" Sookie asks, annoyed. No, Lorelai meant her baby box of mementos from the night Rory was born—much sweeter and nowhere near as Orwellian as the book. In this dystopian novel, Orwell famously introduced the concept of Big Brother, and the phrase has since come to mean invasive government surveillance. How did reading this decades-old book make you feel about where our current technology and administrative oversight capabilities are?

Valley of the Dolls
(1966) BY JACQUELINE SUSANN

Lorelai has just slept with Digger Stiles (er, he prefers to be called Jason now), and in a humiliation even Carrie Bradshaw didn't have to endure, Jason asks her to spend the night in the guest room because he's a light sleeper. He shows her around the room, and Lorelai begrudgingly admits he has "nice taste" in books when he refers to both *Valley of the Dolls* and *Wuthering Heights* as classics. (We already know Lorelai likes this book, because in season 1, she makes a crack that Babette's pill cabinet looks "like a scene from the kitty version of *Valley of the Dolls*" as she clears out the recently departed Cinnamon's medications.) Both the bestselling novel and the movie that came out the following year follow three women as they navigate careers, relationships, sex, drugs, affairs, drugs, sex—did we mention drugs and sex? What do you think of this book? Does it fit into a "classics" category for you, the way it (sarcastically) did for Jason?

Wuthering Heights
(1847) BY EMILY BRONTË

A classic, dark tale of passion, revenge, haunting, and the power structure of Victorian socioeconomic standing. Heathcliff, the main protagonist, is a much-debated literary character. Do you view him as a jilted victim of love, or as a selfish antagonist who deserved the pain he endured?

The Old Man and the Sea
(1952) BY ERNEST HEMINGWAY

Likely another read for Rory's literature class, *The Old Man and the Sea*, much like "The Snows of Kilimanjaro," is another Hemingway title that involves an old man reflecting on his life, but unlike Harry, Santiago ventures out to try his luck again with more determination and perseverance than before. How would you compare the two stories? During the battle of wills between Santiago and the marlin, the fisherman begins to respect the strength and endurance of the fish. What life lessons could a college freshman pull from this text?

Lies and the Lying Liars Who Tell Them

(2003) BY AL FRANKEN

Jess is back in Stars Hollow, and Rory keeps running into him, despite her best efforts. On this occasion he was sitting in an aisle of the bookstore reading this political parody by former *Saturday Night Live* writer and performer and future US senator Al Franken. Do you ever lounge in bookstores and read books before deciding whether or not to buy them?

The Gnostic Gospels

(1979) BY ELAINE PAGELS

If the inclusion of this book feels a little inside-baseball, it's because it is. The title of this episode is "The Nag Hammadi is Where they Found the Gnostic Gospels," which explains a very arcane joke that went over everyone's head at Richard and Emily's Rare Manuscript Acquisition Foundation fundraising dinner. Why was the Nag Hammadi important? Because that's where the Gnostic Gospels were found!

Backstory: These ancient manuscripts were found accidentally in 1945 in a town about seven hours south of Cairo and sold on the black market before they became known to the Egyptian government and scholars worldwide. The thirteen volumes of Coptic texts dated to the mid-fourth century, and they renewed interest in the mostly forgotten and vilified sect of Gnostic Christianity. For those in the rare manuscripts business, this find was monumental. What kind of discovery would be similarly extraordinary in your line of work? After reading these non-canonical gospels, do you think they add to or detract from the church's "official" gospels (meaning Matthew, Mark, Luke, and John)?

> VOCAB: *Gnostic.* Comes from the Greek *gnosis*, meaning "knowledge." In terms of religion, it refers to esoteric or mystical knowledge of the divine. It is the opposite of *agnostic*.

The Andy Warhol Diaries
(1991) EDITED BY PAT HACKETT

As Lane packs up her childhood room in order to move out, her cousin Christine chatters away about Led Zeppelin and the White Stripes and being so impressed with Lane hiding stuff under her floorboards. Poor Lane is so frustrated with her situation that she shuts her younger cousin down and keeps putting books like *The Andy Warhol Diaries* in her moving boxes. This tome of bon mots and trivial (but hilarious) insults is a window into a particular late-'70s/early-'80s era, fantastically told through Warhol's self-absorption and nonstop partying. Were you a fan of Warhol before reading this book? What are your thoughts on him after?

Alice's Adventures in Wonderland

(1865) BY LEWIS CARROLL

Richard's mother, Lorelai the First, a.k.a Trix, has died, and Lorelai is trying to hold her parents' fragile emotional states together. When Jason stops by to offer his condolences, he says he didn't realize Lorelai would be there. "Oh, yeah, well, the white rabbit ran by. I chased him, fell down a hole, and here I am," she replies. The term *following the white rabbit* has come to mean following one odd clue or path and finding oneself in an extraordinary situation. Of course, it's not odd that Lorelai would be at her parents' home, but the state of each of her parents (Richard overwhelmed with grief, and Emily in a drunken fury after finding an old letter Trix sent Richard telling him to leave Emily at the altar because she didn't think she'd make a suitable Gilmore) is definitely an unbelievable circumstance. Have you ever felt like you followed a white rabbit?

Of the many times *Alice's Adventures in Wonderland* is referenced on *Gilmore Girls*, this was probably the funniest: in the wake of Trix's death, Richard is in a catatonic stupor. He keeps asking for "turtleneck soup," a thing his mother made him as a child, but only Sookie figures out he means "mock turtle soup." Of course, mock turtle soup is a real dish, and Carroll's Mock Turtle was a pun based on the popular Victorian meal, and *Gilmore Girls* managed to take his original joke and further spin it. Did you know what Emily was talking about when she first mentioned Richard was asking for turtleneck soup? Is there a particular dish from your childhood that you loved but others would have trouble reconstructing for you?

Larousse Gastronomique
(2001 EDITION) EDITED BY PROSPER MONTAGNÉ

This is the book Sookie pulls from her shelf to find the mock turtle soup recipe. It's a classic in the cooking world—in its numerous editions since 1938, it covers all the necessary techniques, tools, terms, and recipes to create all the sauces and dishes the French are known for. Mock turtle soup, however, is a distinctly English dish, but in its reprintings starting in the 1980s, the cookbook began adding global fare. Have you—or would you—try mock turtle soup? Before looking it up, did you know its primary ingredients?

The Crimson Petal and the White

(2002) BY MICHEL FABER

In Emily's rage over finding the letter Trix sent Richard the night before their wedding, she has fully given up on making "that woman" happy—and that includes following her obnoxiously dictated funeral requests. When Lorelai returns, Emily is in a nightgown, smoking, drinking mojitos, and reading "about this prostitute named Sugar in Victorian England" who "starts rising through the ranks of society" where she "meets these *really vivid characters*!" as Emily tells it. Sugar is contrasted with Agnes, the Victorian feminine ideal who is married to William, an upper-class man who purchases Sugar from her madame and sets her up in her own flat as his mistress. Though it was a recent release, its setting and literary qualities had a distinctly modern Dickensian vibe. Is this the kind of book you would choose to read if you were so blindly angry at your lover that you were getting day drunk and ignoring major family business?

Monsieur Proust
(2003) BY CÉLESTE ALBARET
(TRANSLATED BY BARBARA BRAY)

Always a fan of Proust, Rory brought this biographical account of his last years as told by his beloved house-keeper and trusted companion, Céleste Albaret, with her to Florida on spring break. Albaret refused to speak publicly about her former employer for decades, but in 1972, fifty years after his death, she finally committed her experiences running his middle-of-the-night errands and tiptoeing around so as not to disturb his creative silence to posterity. Does seeing an author's creative process from this wholly different perspective enhance or alter your reading of his work? What were your favorite revelations from Albaret's very upstairs/downstairs account of her famous employer?

The Price of Loyalty: George W. Bush, the White House, and the Education of Paul O'Neill

(2004) BY RON SUSKIND

Rory also brought this *New York Times* bestseller, which took a critical look at the events leading up to the Iraq War from the perspective and detailed documentation of Paul O'Neill—Bush's treasury secretary for his first two years in office—to the beach during spring break. What books do you like to read on vacation?

The Trial
(1925) BY FRANZ KAFKA

Rory is taking a contemporary political fiction course, taught by Professor Asher Fleming, a former Yale class-mate of Richard's and a revered novelist. Professor Fleming assigns this work, saying they'll discuss neglect of the individual as a hallmark of modern government in the next class. Published posthumously, Kafka's *Trial* fol-lows a man arrested and accused of a crime, though he is not told exactly what his offense was, and the absurdity of the trial that follows. How did you feel while reading this book? Do you think there are any parallels between the way Kafka's protagonist, Josef, is treated and current-day proceedings regarding justice and the law? Would you consider oppressive bureaucracy, such as Josef was unsuc-cessfully navigating, a "hallmark of modern government," the way Kafka did?

SEASON 5

Wherein Rory and Lorelai disagree about Rory's sleeping with Dean, leading to Rory going to Europe with Emily for the summer; Rory attempts a casual relationship with wealthy playboy Logan Huntzberger, but they soon become exclusive; Richard and Emily are thrilled with Logan because he's from an important society family, but Logan's family strongly disapproves of Rory; Luke and Lorelai start a serious relationship; Richard and Emily reunite and renew their vows; Emily tells Christopher he should try to win back Lorelai, causing a separation with Luke and a major rift between Lorelai and Emily; Rory decides to quit Yale; Lorelai asks her parents to help her convince Rory to stay in school, but instead they enable to her quit and allow her to move into their pool house; Lorelai is on the outs with Rory, Richard, and Emily; when Luke is supportive of Lorelai, she proposes to him.

The Breaker
(1998) BY MINETTE WALTERS

This contemporary crime thriller, which searches for a murderer after a woman washes up on a Dorset shore, doesn't immediately seem like Rory's cup of tea, but it was the book sitting on her bedside table as she and Dean cuddled post-sex. Perhaps she was trying a few new things? Are there any books that you would be embarrassed to have a lover see on your nightstand?

Daisy Miller
(1879) BY HENRY JAMES

Lorelai is actively upset about Rory's choice to sleep with a married Dean, and when Emily offers Rory the chance to go to Europe with her for the summer, she pushes her into it. "What is this, a Henry James novel?" Rory asks her mother. "The young lady acts up and her family ships her off to Europe? Say goodbye to Daisy Miller!" The eponymous American heroine wasn't quite shipped off because of a scandal, but she did cause quite a few while vacationing in Switzerland and Italy one summer. Similar to how Lorelai managed to separate Rory and Dean for the summer, people tried to convince Daisy to separate from her Italian fling when their flirtatiousness created a scandal among the ex-pats in Rome. How would you handle this kind of news, if you found out a friend was having an affair? Have you had to deal with a situation like this before?

The Da Vinci Code

(2003) BY DAN BROWN

At Luke's, Brian prattles excitedly about the background lore behind *The Da Vinci Code*, which Zack doesn't remotely care about. The blockbuster book spent more than two years atop the *New York Times* bestseller list, and suddenly everyone was a Robert Langdon–level expert/conspiracy theorist on Catholic Templars. Who else in Stars Hollow do you think Brian could have talked about this book with? Who would have sided with Zack?

The Pursuit of Love
(1945)
Love in a Cold Climate
(1949) BY NANCY MITFORD

These two postwar novels were the ones that put Nancy Mitford, socialite and eldest of the infamous Mitford sisters, on the literary map. She based the large, fictitious Radlett family on her own and satirizes the British upper classes throughout both stories. Considering how well-known the various members of Mitford's family were (Nancy's other sisters regularly made headlines for their extremist political views—one was a communist, one a fascist, and one a Nazi—and one was a well-liked British duchess), do you think these books fared well because they pulled from her family at large? Does knowing this make you want to read more about the real-life sisters, or do Nancy's novels stand on their own?

The Anarchist Cookbook
(1971) BY WILLIAM POWELL

Glenn, one of the writers at the *Yale Daily News*, gets a byline in the *New York Times* when they publish his review of the reprinting of *The Anarchist Cookbook*, a highly litigious book written by a teenager after he was drafted into the Vietnam War. The book contains "recipes" for various guerilla warfare techniques, like how to throw a perfect Molotov cocktail, how to turn a shotgun into a grenade launcher, and how to build DIY explosives. This book has been banned in the United Kingdom and Australia, and police have linked the book to a number of high-profile domestic terrorism attacks. In the United States, the FBI concluded that it falls under First Amendment protection. Do you agree, either in theory or in practice?

The Curious Incident of the Dog in the Night-time

(2003) BY MARK HADDON

Rory was carrying this award-winning mystery novel when she approached Logan on campus to ask for his input on her article about the Life and Death Brigade, a Yale secret society that she's pretty positive he's a member of. In the book, the child protagonist sets out to solve a couple of mysteries, similar to how Rory is setting out on her first bit of investigative reporting. If you were in Rory's shoes, how heavy-handed would you have been with Logan? Would you have gone on the Life and Death Brigade trip with him? Why or why not?

NO MORE ICED TEAS, NORMAN MAILER!

The Dragonfly Inn is still new to town, but it has already become a budding literary hotspot. Norman Mailer, the famously cantankerous journalist and novelist who had been both venerated and vilified over the course of his long career, set up shop in the dining room during lunch hour, apparently for many days in a row. Lorelai is thrilled. "This is our first step on the road to being saloned!" she tells Sookie. "It's just a matter of time before the rest of the literati come sweeping in."

Sookie, on the other hand, is not so keen on his being there. While she prepares full lunches each day, he takes up a large table and only orders iced tea. And with their new-business budget already strained and lunch being the obvious short-term cut, Sookie is convinced this is Norman Mailer's fault. After blowing up at him and removing the iced tea from his table, she realizes why she's been feeling crazy. "Norman Mailer!" she yells before hugging him, "I'm pregnant!"

- *The Naked and the Dead* (1948) by Norman Mailer
- *The Armies of the Night: History as a Novel, the Novel as History* (1968) by Norman Mailer
- *The Executioner's Song* (1979) by Norman Mailer

Three of Mailer's most famous books lay on the table, including his first novel, *The Naked and the Dead*, which was published when he was twenty-five. His first nonfiction work, *The Armies of the Night*, and *The Executioner's Song*, a true crime novel, both won Pulitzer Prizes, making Mailer the only person ever to win a Pulitzer in both the fiction and nonfiction categories.

Each of these books approaches a historical event from a different angle. *The Naked and the Dead*, which Lorelai claims Rory read while still in footsie pajamas, is a novel based on Mailer's firsthand accounts of being stationed in the Philippines during the last months of World War II. (Pretty heavy reading for a toddler, even for Rory!) *The Armies of the Night*, a hallmark example of New Journalism, has Mailer reporting on the 1967 March on the Pentagon to protest the Vietnam War. *The Executioner's Song* is a true-crime novel based on extensive interviews with a convicted murderer who became the first man executed in the United States in over a decade, after the Supreme Court reinstated the death penalty. Which of these books was your favorite? Which style—the novel, the nonfiction, or the true crime novel—did you find the most satisfactory?

FUN FACT: The reporter who is interviewing Mailer at the inn is his real-life son Stephen Mailer.

The Iliad
AND
The Odyssey
(8TH CENTURY BCE) BY HOMER

After a day spent on the golf course with Richard, a tipsy Luke calls Lorelai from the driving range, rambling about all the financial decisions Richard has made for him and his diner, and how now he needs to read *The Iliad* and *The Odyssey* because he "sort of implied" he's fond of the Greeks, so now Richard wants to chat about these two classics. Luckily for Luke, who seems to enjoy a good war story, *The Iliad* is about the tail end of the Trojan War, one of the most famous wars in history. *The Odyssey* is about a Greek hero's long journey home. Do you think, if Luke could get over the dactylic hexameter thing, that he would enjoy these mythologized war stories? Who were your favorite characters in these books, the gods or the mortals?

The Scarlet Letter
(1850) BY NATHANIEL HAWTHORNE

It's time for the annual Revolutionary War Battle of Stars Hollow reenactment, and this year there's excitement because new research shows a "brave lady of the town used her wiles" to intercept and otherwise occupy a British general, giving the rebels a chance to ambush his awaiting army. One man wants to call this new reenactor role "the scarlet woman," which Andrew, the town's bookseller, called "too Nathaniel Hawthorne." In Hawthorne's *The Scarlet Letter*, set during Puritan colonial times, no one would have praised its scarlet woman, Hester Prynne, as a brave lady, even though concealing the identity of her child's father through extreme public shaming was certainly brave. What name would you have given the Stars Hollow heroine?

An Enquiry Concerning the Principles of Morals
(1751) BY DAVID HUME

After a discussion on Hume's proposition that morals stem from self-love, Rory's professor says they'll continue deliberating his positions during the next class. In this book, Hume argues that our individual moral senses play a greater role in judgments about vice-versus-virtues than logic or reason do. Do you agree with him or not? Does this stance allow for different cultures or religions to have differing opinions on what is moral and what isn't? Do you find that in itself morally problematic, or as it should be?

THE CASE OF THE SCHOOLGIRL CRUSH

⸺◇◇◇◇◇⸺

When Doyle panics about getting pressure from Logan's newspaper magnate father about making sure his son is getting bylines, Rory offers to give Logan a bunch of her research to help him on a story. When they meet up, he tries to get to know her a bit better and convinces her to stay for a drink. When she asks about his father's connection to Seymour Hersh and mentions that she read *My Lai 4* when she was twelve, Logan looks appropriately

astonished. "You read a book about the My Lai massacre when you were twelve?" he asks, making sure he heard her correctly. "Well, I polished off Nancy Drew that year too," Rory replies, as if to show she was still a typical preteen.

- *My Lai 4: A Report on the Massacre and Its Aftermath* (1970) by Seymour M. Hersh
- *The Nancy Drew Series* (1930–1979) by Carolyn Keene

Did you ever read books considered atypical for your age? Do you remember what you were reading, watching, or obsessed with at age twelve? And did you finish any particular series of books, such as Nancy Drew, as a young reader? Did that fuel a love of a particular genre later on?

A Heartbreaking Work
of Staggering Genius
(2000) BY DAVE EGGERS

Dave Eggers's debut memoir details a young adulthood thrown out of balance by the sudden demands of parenthood. At age twenty, Eggers's parents died within weeks of each other, and he became the primary caregiver and guardian of his eight-year-old brother. The book has a tragic backdrop, but over the course of the sometimes hilarious and often insightful story, the reader follows two young boys as they figure out growing up together. We see Rory, who is roughly the age Eggers was when he became a surrogate parent, reading this book late one night. How did you feel while reading this book? Did you or someone you know have to "grow up too soon" because of a family tragedy? How did that shape yours or their perspective on life?

Leaves of Grass
(1855) BY WALT WHITMAN

When Richard and Emily return from their trip to Greece, they bring Rory a gift: the book *Leaves of Grass*, in Greek. Richard gushes over its beautiful, hundred-year-old engravings and leather binding, and Rory quips that now she'll need to learn Greek. Perhaps we can assume her grandparents chose this book because it was one she already liked, but why would this volume in particular be in a Greek antique bookstore? Unlike some authors, Walt Whitman traveled outside of his native New York region only a few times, and he left the country—for a two-month trip to Canada—only once. But to his contemporaries, he and his philosophies were as Greek as they came.

"Walt Whitman is more truly Greek than any other man of modern times," John Addington Symonds wrote in his 1873 work *Studies of the Greek Poets*. "Hopeful and fearless, accepting the world as he finds it, recognizing the value of each human impulse, shirking no obligations, self-regulated by a law of perfect health, he, in the midst of a chaotic age, emerges clear and distinct, at one with nature, and therefore Greek."

Do you see this connection between ancient Greek philosophy and writing when reading Whitman? Whitman, who was famously very *meh* on Shakespeare, preferred the drama of ancient Greece as well. "As depicter and dramatist of the passions, Shakespeare is equal'd by several, and excelled by the best old Greeks—as Aeschylus," he once wrote a friend. Do you agree with Whitman? Or do you think he's comparing apples to olives?

STILL IN HER
RUSSIAN PHASE

———◇◇◇◇◇———

Rory gets a job at Stars Hollow Books doing inventory over spring break, and when Lane pops in to see her, she has a full system in place: a pile of need-to-inventory, a pile of inventoried, and a "pile of books that I've seen and now have to buy." As Lane notes, this job must be costing her a fortune.

Of the dozen or so books she's set aside for herself, the two that are most visible are definitely in the Rory wheelhouse: books by or about the Russian greats.

Demons (1872) by Fyodor Dostoevsky

Written during a period of social and economic upheaval, Dostoevsky's *Demons* deals with the perceived evils of "-isms": idealism, socialism, nihilism, atheism, etc. In the early 1850s, Dostoevsky himself spent four years in a Siberian hard-labor camp because of his participation in the Petrashevsky Circle, a group of progressive intellectuals who opposed the tsarist autocracy and serfdom; twenty years later, a new tsar had emancipated the serfs, but taxes remained so high and viable livelihoods so scant that peasants and the lowest classes were on the verge of another uprising and one of an eventual four assassination attempts had been made on Tsar Alexander II. Do you think knowing historical context like this makes novels more realistic or easier to understand? How often do you look up information about the time and place a book was written in to see if you can glean additional context?

Pushkin: A Biography (2002) by T. J. Binyon

Alexander Pushkin, considered the founder of modern Russian literature, was a beacon of Russian poetry and art during his lifetime. It's been said that Pushkin is in the blood of Russians the way Shakespeare is in the English. Did this biography convince you of that idea? Who is your favorite national poet? Is there a particular poet or author you think truly defines your country? Your state?

Angels in America

(1991) BY TONY KUSHNER

After seeing a play that Logan groaned through, Rory chides him for not enjoying theater more. She mentions seeing *Caroline, or Change* with her mom and how it was amazing, then notes that it's Tony Kushner's musical— you know, Tony Kushner who wrote *Angels in America*. "I know who Tony Kushner is," Logan humblebrags. "My mom plays canasta with him." Do you find it endearing or annoying that Logan is so blasé about the famous writers and artists who run in his parents' circle? Do you find it odd that Rory just brushes off Logan's nonchalance about his proximity to them, or do you think that she just sees it as part of his charm?

Social Origins of Dictatorship and Democracy: Lord and Peasant in the Making of the Modern World

(1966) BY BARRINGTON MOORE, JR.

"No bourgeois, no democracy." That's the most concise way to boil down Moore's primary argument from this classic social science text, which Rory is seen casually reading in the dining hall. Moore studied how various counties evolved politically after they were industrialized. He argues that the type of political system (democratic, fascist, or communist) a country arrived at after it modernized depended on the relationship between the landed and working classes, using countries like the United States, England, France, China, Japan, and Russia as example. After reading Moore's thesis, do you agree with it? What do you see as other primary factors as to how political systems are implemented or maintained in countries?

INN READS

———◇◇◇◇◇———

Lorelai has lovingly created a relaxing library for guests at the Dragonfly, with shelves and cabinets full of classic leather-bound books by the likes of Jonathan Swift, Edith Wharton, and Charles Dickens. But she's dismayed when she discovers that one shelf now has *Clifford the Big Red Dog* and five copies of *He's Just Not That Into You*; as Sookie says, they've been "airplane booked." Have you ever left behind reading materials at inns or Airbnbs so that you don't have to travel home with them? Have you ever read or leafed through a book simply because it was left in a lobby or bookshelf, even if it wasn't your typical fare? And would you (or have you) ever taken a nicer volume from an inn because you thought it was up for grabs?

- *He's Just Not That Into You* (2004) by Greg Behrendt and Liz Tuccillo
- *Clifford the Big Red Dog* (1963) by Norman Bridwell

Ethics

(2000) BY BARUCH SPINOZA
(TRANSLATED BY G. H. R. PARKINSON)

Rory's ethics class is moving on from the empiricists to the rationalists, and her professor asks the group to get started on *Ethics*, by the Dutch philosopher and Enlightenment-era rationalist Spinoza. When Spinoza was just twenty-three, he was expelled from his Portuguese Jewish community in Amsterdam for his "heretical" views; he argued against the idea that God directly handed laws to men, that "God" and "Nature" were one in the same, and that humans, as part of nature, must follow the same basic principles as everything else in nature. Do you agree or disagree with Spinoza's assessments? Why?

HOW TO MAKE A
GOOD IMPRESSION

———◇◇◇◇———

After Logan's newspaper magnate father offers Rory an internship, she excitedly begins researching everything she can find on him and his interests. Among those findings were that he covered Haiti in the eighties and wrote a wine column at one point, so she decides to do a weekend cram session on these topics, just in case. Logan, who seems to know nothing about his father beyond his dislike of peas, tells her she's learned more about his father in one day than he has in his whole life.

- *Haiti: State Against Nation* (1990) by
  Michel-Rolph Trouillot
- *Written in Blood: The Story of the Haitian People 1492–1995*
  (1996) by Robert Debs Heinl and Nancy Gordon Heinl
- *Larousse Encyclopedia of Wine* (1994) by
  Christopher Foulkes
- *The Wine Bible* (2000) by Karen MacNeil

Do you think Rory's extreme research strategy is a good one? How much research have you ever done beforehand on a potential boss or colleague?

SEASON 6

Wherein Rory and Lorelai are not on speaking terms because Rory has quit Yale and moved into her grandparents' pool house; Lorelai adopts a dog named Paul Anka; Emily gets Rory a job at the DAR; Rory decides to return to Yale after Jess admonishes her for wasting her potential; Christopher comes into a large inheritance and takes over paying for Yale, angering Richard and Emily; Luke learns he has a twelve-year-old daughter, April, and works to get to know her; after postponing their wedding while Luke got to know April, Lorelai issues an ultimatum that he elope with her; Luke is flustered and says he can't elope, so Lorelai ends their relationship.

The Lion, the Witch and the Wardrobe

(1950) BY C. S. LEWIS

The Gilmore girls have never seemed to be ones to espouse religion—they both have a strong moral compass, but the only times we've seen them inside the town church were for funerals. But when Sookie asked Lorelai and Rory to be the godmothers to her two children, Davey and Martha, the reverend, who has known them for years, sits them down to ask what their religious affiliations are. Lorelei replies that she has a strong belief in good over evil, and Rory chimes in that she read *The Lion, the Witch and the Wardrobe* before. While C. S. Lewis denied that he'd written this first volume of his Chronicles of Narnia series as a children's theological novel, it has been viewed and analyzed as a Christian allegorical tale since publication. If you read this book as a child, did you pick up on the biblical references? Do you see them when reading it now?

Primary Colors
(1996) BY JOE KLEIN

While trying to get a job at the *Stamford Eagle Gazette*, Rory suggests using language analysis software to pinpoint a person who was sending anonymous letters, noting that this was how Joe Klein was unmasked as the author of *Primary Colors*. The book was a very thinly veiled fictional account of Bill Clinton's 1992 presidential campaign, and Klein was a well-known *Newsweek* columnist who opted to publish the novel anonymously because he didn't want it to be judged as the work of "Joe Klein, the journalist." Considering Rory wants to be seen as a serious journalist, do you think she would ever contemplate making a similar choice—especially given the extremely famous campaign trail she heads off to cover after graduation?

Beowulf: A New Verse Translation

(1999) BY SEAMUS HEANEY

Rory recommended this award-winning new translation of the medieval Old English epic poem to her mother, who said she quit reading it after three minutes. *Beowulf* follows a Scandinavian prince as he slays the monster Grendel, and then must confront Grendel's mother, the even-more-terrifying seahag. Heaney's translation was praised not only because he, as a poet, could recreate the rhythm of the original but also because his Irish language and dialect gave a new level of accessibility to the ancient writing. Why do you think Rory recommended this famously difficult elegiac work to her mother? Do you ever recommend books to your parents or friends? How do they respond to your suggestions?

The Best of
Martha Stewart
Living: Holidays

(1993) BY MARTHA STEWART LIVING

While Liz tries making Thanksgiving dinner in Luke's apartment, she keeps referring to this work by the Queen of Domestic Arts ("She knows everything," Liz asserts). Luke tells Liz to get some canned cranberry sauce since her homemade one didn't even turn out red—have you ever had a recipe go completely awry? What favorite recipes have you found in collections like this?

It Takes a Village
(1996) BY HILLARY CLINTON

As Paris shows Rory her new digs, she quips that she only bothered to meet two of her neighbors because that was "enough *It Takes a Village*" for her. How many neighbors do you think Rory—who could be considered a poster child for the *It Takes a Village* philosophy—got to know once she moved in?

One Day in the Life of Ivan Denisovich
(1962) BY ALEKSANDR SOLZHENITSYN

Is anyone surprised that Paris immediately morphs into a totalitarian editrix (*totalitariatrix*?) when she takes over the chief position at the *Yale Daily News*? As she informs Rory, "Journalism is an art form, and the best art is created under repression, like Stalin's gulag." Her proof? This novella, written by a Nobel Prize winner who, just like the title character, did spend many years in a Soviet work camp. Do you agree with Paris? What other popular works have been written or created under such harsh circumstances? Have you ever had a boss or superior with a mindset like Paris? If so, how did your work succeed or suffer?

Angela's Ashes

(1996) BY FRANK McCOURT

Lorelai calls Paris's apartment *"Angela's Ashes"* as short-hand to convey how "sad" and dilapidated she thought it was. McCourt's bestselling memoir detailed his childhood living in abject poverty in both Brooklyn and Limerick, Ireland, whereas the apartment Rory moved into with Paris just had a lot of locks on the door and some unsightly water damage on the walls. We know Lorelai struggled for many years when Rory was young, so why do you think she'd have such an Emily-esque reaction to an apartment that was simply a bit downtrodden? Did you ever have apartments in college or later that your family thought weren't nice enough?

173

The Big Love
(2004) BY SARAH DUNN

As Lorelai cleans up a book cabinet that Paul Anka made a mess of, we can see a few of her book choices strewn about. This debut novel from television writer Sarah Dunn (who later worked on Amy Sherman-Palladino's post–*Gilmore Girls* show *Bunheads*) is about a late bloomer who's out in the dating world again after her boyfriend runs out for dinner-party condiments and never returns. She ruminates over all the reasons that relationship ended, has an office fling that ends poorly, and tries to work through a lifetime of faith, trust, and commitment issues. *The Big Love* feels very much like a juicy beach read that Lorelai would devour in an afternoon.

The Sisters:
The Saga of the Mitford Family
(2002) BY MARY S. LOVELL

The six infamous Mitford sisters were prominent aristocratic British socialites in the 1920s and '30s, half of whom produced particularly scandalous headlines. One journalist described them as "Diana the Fascist, Jessica the Communist, Unity the Hitler-lover, Nancy the Novelist, Deborah the Duchess, and Pamela the unobtrusive poultry connoisseur." This biography was also in the pile of Lorelai's books—which of the sisters do you think she found most interesting, and why?

Robert's Rules of Order
(1876) BY HENRY ROBERT

If you've attended any kind of official government meeting, sat on a school board or board of directors, held rank in a sorority or fraternity, etc., you likely have a broad understanding of *Robert's Rules of Order* (which, *of course* Paris would lecture the newsroom staff on in a fit of pique). Originally titled *Pocket Manual of Rules of Order for Deliberative Assemblies*, the set of guidelines was laid out in 1876 by US Army officer Henry M. Roberts. Rules like the order of motions, quorums for voting, and being recognized by the chair before speaking are all basic principles of *Robert's Rules*. Which of these do you think make the most sense? Do any feel particularly out of date to you?

All the Pretty Horses
(1992) BY CORMAC McCARTHY

This western novel follows a pair of sixteen-year-old cow-boys as they leave Texas for Mexico, looking for work and adventure. The boys are strong and brave enough to fend for themselves but also young and naïve enough to not understand the consequences of many of their more questionable choices. Logan is reading this at home when Rory brings her dad into their newly shared apartment for the first time. Do you think any of Logan's actions or attributes mirror those of John Grady, the novel's protag-onist? In what ways does Logan act like an adult and in what ways is he still childish?

The Year of Magical Thinking
(2005) BY JOAN DIDION

Didion had long been a famous journalist and screen-writer when she wrote this deadpan yet uplifting memoir—which Rory was reading on her Valentine's weekend Martha's Vineyard getaway with Logan, her mother, and Luke—about some of the most awful and heartbreaking things that could happen in one's life. In Didion's typical style, she self-examines while avoiding oversentimentality. What do you think Rory likes or appreciates about Didion's writing? Do you think you would be able to conjure perspective the way Didion did in this book if similar events (the near-death of a child, the death of a spouse) happened to you?

Joan Didion is considered one of the pioneers of New Journalism—essentially writing perspective-based long-form nonfiction—along with Tom Wolfe, Hunter S. Thompson, and Gay Talese. Do you think this more narrative form of journalistic writing is something Rory should consider? Do you think it would fit her writing strengths? Why or why not?

Brideshead Revisited
(1945) BY EVELYN WAUGH

This beloved British tragicomedy doesn't technically make an appearance in *Gilmore Girls*, but like *The Gnostic Gospels*, the joke is in the episode's title: "Bridesmaids Revisited." Logan's sister, Honor, is getting married, and though Rory and Logan were just on the outs a few episodes ago, she hangs out in the bridal suite with Honor and her many promiscuous bridesmaids. She learns that Logan recently slept with three of the four of them, and when she confronts him about it, he pulls a Ross Geller: "We were on a break!" How would you have reacted if you were in Rory's shoes?

Harry Potter series
(1997–2007) BY J. K. ROWLING

After Luke returns from chaperoning April's field trip to Philadelphia, Anna informs him that he was such a hit with the busload of teen girls that they've begun affectionately referring to him as Hagrid. "Very big, very hairy, very love-able," she explains, in perhaps one of the sweetest references aimed squarely at millennials. "It's a huge compliment."

It's probably safe to assume that April had read all six of the eventual seven novels that had come out at the time this episode aired. Did you read the series when it came out, or were you slightly older or younger when they were released? Did you read Harry Potter before or after seeing the movies? Do you think this series will continue to be as culturally important to future generations as it was for the kids who grew up waiting for each new Potter release?

- *Harry Potter and the Sorcerer's Stone* (1997)
- *Harry Potter and the Chamber of Secrets* (1998)
- *Harry Potter and the Prisoner of Azkaban* (1999)
- *Harry Potter and the Goblet of Fire* (2000)
- *Harry Potter and the Order of the Phoenix* (2003)
- *Harry Potter and the Half-Blood Prince* (2005)
- *Harry Potter and the Deathly Hallows* (2007)

Harold and the Purple Crayon

(1955) BY CROCKETT JOHNSON

April tells Lorelai that this is one of her favorite books, even though she knows she's too old for it. What books from your early childhood have stuck with you like this? Do you also love anything in particular—the way April is partial to purple—that you can pinpoint to a childhood obsession?

The New Way Things Work

(1998) BY DAVID MACAULAY

For a smart, curious girl like April, this book of fun diagrams explaining actual mechanics and scientific principles would be a great birthday gift (kudos to Lorelai for nixing Luke's terrible cat-covered toiletry kit idea). Also, this seems like a book Luke, who is great at building and craftsmanship, would be able to bond with his daughter over. What birthday gifts do you remember as stand-out items you loved? What were some of the lamest gifts? And what are your go-tos for children, based on things you've seen be hits or misses?

The Red Badge of Courage
(1895) BY STEPHEN CRANE

The title refers to a teen soldier's desire for a visible injury after his shame and guilt at having fled a battlefield during the Civil War. But within the context of the episode, Lorelai and Sookie reminisce about how fun playing with makeup was when they were April's age, when it was all wet n wild eyeliner and Bonne Bell Lip Smackers. Somewhere during this teen girl memory-fest, Sookie says that a boy actually ate her chocolate fudge–flavored Lip Smacker and then threw it up all over her copy of *The Red Badge of Courage*. Do you have a classic book that you associate with some completely different personal story along these lines?

Stalin:
The Court of the Red Tsar
(2003) BY SIMON SEBAG MONTEFIORE

When Rory refuses to stop taking photos of Logan on his graduation day, he jokingly says he needs to "take that Stalin biography away from you." Odds are that Rory has read a number of Stalin biographies, but this particular one was a fairly recent bestseller that she could have added to her "to purchase" pile at the bookstore. Of the many eras of Russian history and literature that Rory has read, which do you think she likes the most? Which have you found most interesting?

LORELAI'S ESSENTIAL READS

For all the book and culture references Rory and Lorelai trade back and forth, *Gilmore Girls* features a number of sweet mother/daughter moments where they just lounge at home, reading their respective books. Lorelai's tastes trend toward nostalgia and the entertainingly salacious, though her prep school years clearly gave her a strong grounding in the classics.

Kitchen Confidential: Adventures in the Culinary Underbelly (2000) by Anthony Bourdain (season 1, episode 4)

Chef Anthony Bourdain was the type of writer who could make non-foodies care deeply about food, and this book, which was released just two months before the episode aired, sets the scene for just the type of juicy, unfiltered, insider-y memoir we'd come to expect from Lorelai's bookshelf. Do you enjoy learning about the background gossip and culture for a specific space like a fast-paced, high-end restaurant kitchen? If you could be a fly on the wall of one of your favorite restaurants, which would you choose? What would you hope to learn?

The Dirt: Confessions of the World's Most Notorious Rock Band (2001) by Mötley Crüe and Neil Strauss (season 2, episode 18)

Following the highs and lows of one of L.A.'s most hedonistic and outrageous metal bands, *The Dirt* is a compilation autobiography by the band's infamous members Tommy Lee, Mick Mars, Vince Neil, and Nikki Sixx, and Lorelai *loves* it. "I swear, you get to the point where Ozzy Osbourne snorts a row of ants and you think it cannot get any grosser. And then, you turn the page, and *oh hello, yes it can*! It's excellent!" she tells Rory. Do you enjoy these kinds of behind-the-scenes looks at famously libertine bands? Which band or artist autobiography have you enjoyed the most or are waiting to be released?

Deenie (1973) by Judy Blume (season 3, episode 6)

When Lorelai reveals that she was reading this book around the time she had Rory, it feels like a nail hit right on the head. Judy Blume's oft-banned coming-of-age story concerns thirteen-year-old Deenie, who is saddled with a back brace and the crushing weight of her mother's plans for her future. How much of herself do you think she saw in Deenie? Have you ever felt that pressure in your own life from your parents or family? How did you handle it?

Flowers in the Attic (1979) by V. C. Andrews (season 3, episode 7)

As Sookie panics over Jackson's recent revelation of wanting "four in four"—i.e., four kids in four years—Lorelai tries to give her friend the courage to tell her new husband that that's way too many kids on too tight a time frame. "You can't just stick four kids in the attic and pull them out at Christmas!" she says, recalling the basic premise of this popular gothic novel. Of course, locking the four Dollanganger children in the attic resulted in incest, abandonment, and murder, none of which the future Belleville children would need to worry about. This book has Lorelai's Not-So-Guilty Pleasure Read stamped all over it. What guilty-pleasure reads do you have? Which ones are you not remotely embarrassed to admit?

Nickel and Dimed: On (Not) Getting by in America (2001) by Barbara Ehrenreich (season 3, episode 13)

Lorelai, who left a life of comfort and privilege to start out on her own—which included working as a hotel maid and living in the inn's potting shed with her toddler—was reading this in the hospital waiting room while Christopher's second daughter was being born. This work of investigative journalism took the author across the country working a variety of low-wage jobs—waitress, hotel maid, Walmart cashier—all while trying to find affordable housing within her income range. After a year of exhausting physical and mental labor, Ehrenreich wrote about how even the healthiest, hardest workers cannot survive on minimum wage, and how multiple jobs and no time to rest become the norm in order to pay the bills. Have you ever worked low-wage jobs to get by? Did it change your perspective in any way? This book is now more than twenty years old, but do you think it still resonates in the same way? Why or why not?

I'm with the Band: Confessions of a Groupie (1987) by Pamela Des Barres (season 3, episode 16)

Lorelai was in a rock 'n' roll state of mind after helping Lane and her band, Hep Alien, turn her shed into a practice space. Just a couple of episodes after Rory made a Pamela Des Barres reference, Lorelai is lounging around on a weekend, reading Des Barres's memoir of her life in the 1960s and '70s, her time as Frank Zappa's nanny, her relationships with Jimmy Page and Mick Jagger, and her eventual marriage to British glam rocker Michael Des Barres. Besides the Bangles, which Lorelai once told Christopher she planned to follow around the world if she hadn't had Rory, which other bands would Lorelai be a groupie for? Which bands, past or present, would you follow around the world if given the chance?

Sailing Alone Around the Room: New and Selected Poems (2001) by Billy Collins (season 6, episode 16)

Published during his tenure as the Poet Laureate of the United States, Collins's poems are known for their plain language and everyday scenarios and have been called "transparent on the surface yet become . . . ambiguous, thought-provoking . . . once the reader has peered into the depths." Lorelai was reading this at night in bed—do you find poetry a soothing bedtime read? What is your ideal nighttime read?

My Life So Far (2005) by Jane Fonda (season 7, episode 1)

It seems fitting that Lorelai is reading this memoir, as Jane Fonda is just the sort of ambitious, rebellious spirit that she might look up to. After a lifetime of antiwar and pro-feminist activist work, workout videos, and Barbarella pinups, it's easy to forget Fonda also won two Best Actress Oscars and seven Golden Globes. In her hefty autobiography, she breaks her life down into three acts, each of approximately thirty years, and lays out the plan for her third act, which she hopes will be her greatest one yet. Lorelai is solidly in her second act, and she's already accomplished a couple of her biggest goals—namely, opening her own successful inn and raising a daughter who is on the verge of graduating from an Ivy League school. Her love life, however, is in shambles as she's reading Fonda's book. She's just called things off with Luke and slept with Christopher, all in the past twenty-four hours. Have you ever blown up your life overnight like that? Or known someone who has? What kind of books, music, or stories do you turn to to help you through tough times?

SEASON 7

Wherein Lorelai and Luke officially
split when she confesses she slept with
Christopher; Lorelai and Christopher
spontaneously marry while on a trip to
Paris; Rory and Logan are doing a long-
distance relationship while he is in London;
Luke sues for joint custody of April; Lorelai
writes Luke a character reference for his
custody hearing, and he wins; Richard
has a heart attack while lecturing at Yale;
Christopher finds the letter Lorelai wrote,
leading to their divorce; Rory panics over
post-graduation plans; Logan proposes to
Rory, but when she says she can't move to
California with him, he breaks off their
relationship completely; Rory accepts a
job covering Barack Obama's presidential
campaign for an online newspaper; Stars
Hollow throws Rory a farewell party; when
Lorelai learns that Luke put the whole
thing together, she kisses him.

LORELAI'S BREAKUP BOX

———◦◦◇◦◦———

As Lorelai goes through the ritualistic putting-everything-that-reminds-me-of-him-into-a-box routine, Rory sifts through the books Lorelai gave or recommended to Luke that he didn't read. Cormac McCarthy and Truman Capote were among the bunch, and Rory agrees that Luke would have appreciated them. Later, while staring at her now spare living room, Lorelai tries telling herself it's Zen, while Rory responds "Thoreau, Walden pond" (which, coincidently, is another book that Luke would probably love).

- *In Cold Blood* (1965) by Truman Capote
- *Walden* (1854) by Henry David Thoreau

Have you ever gone through this custom of cleansing your space and removing an ex's items, the way we've seen both Lorelai and Rory do? Does it help? Are there books, albums, or other cultural items that you felt that you "lost" in a breakup, because they remind you of that person? Do you think it's possible to reclaim them later?

Charlotte's Web

(1952) BY E. B. WHITE

When Rory mentions that this children's classic is one of her favorite books, Lorelai says, "Spiders talking to pigs, what could be better than that?" Of course, the book is about more than just barnyard hijinks—the theme of friendship and being a true, dependable friend plays a major part throughout the story of Wilbur and Charlotte. As this last season of *Gilmore Girls* gets started, who have been the friends that Lorelai and Rory have been able to depend on the most? Do you think the central premise of the show—that they are two best friends who just happen to be mother and daughter—still stands?

Sexus

(1949) BY HENRY MILLER

Rory is struggling with the long-distance thing with Logan, so when Paris suggests phone sex and sexting, does Rory pull out a *Cosmo* magazine for tips? Nope, she goes straight to Henry Miller. Granted, Miller's semiautobiographical books, including *Sexus*, feature what the *New York Times* called "licentious sex scenes," and many of his works were banned in the United States and abroad because of that.

Meanwhile, Lane is reading *What to Expect When You're Expecting* because instead of consulting any good women's magazines on sex and contraception, she and Zack attempted to recreate the sex-on-the-beach scene in *From Here to Eternity*, and it was awful and they didn't use protection. Just like an afterschool special, Lane got pregnant her first time.

If you were attempting to sext for the first time, would you go to a decades-old book, like Rory did, or something more contemporary, like song lyrics?

Ironweed

(1983) BY WILLIAM KENNEDY

During a fight over a negative story Rory wrote about a networking function he took her to, Logan name-checks this Pulitzer-winning novel while telling Rory that she's not morally superior to trust-fund kids and people who use their connections to get ahead. While Rory thought she was writing a frothy, sardonic piece about a fairly ridiculous event, Logan took it as a personal admonishment of his background and business prospects. In *Ironweed*, the protagonist is trying to survive during the Depression while being haunted by excessive guilt from his past. Do you see the connection Logan was making between his view of Rory's article and this book? Do you think his stance was fair, or that Rory's piece was perfectly fine and he was being overly sensitive? Have you ever written or said something that offended a friend? How did you react to their feelings of hurt or anger?

The Norton Anthologies

While moving Rory back into Paris and Doyle's apartment, her boxes of books are causing everyone grief. "Two copies of the Norton Anthology?" Logan protests, before Rory justifies that they were gifts. To be fair, Norton has published a number of anthologies, including for English Literature, Poetry, Theory and Criticism, Drama, and American Literature—any of which Rory would probably happily consume. But, at over four pounds each, these tomes could add up quickly. Do you like reading or referring to anthologies of similar works, or do you prefer to have individual books for individual works? Do you ever double up?

P IS FOR PREGNANT

—◦◇◇◦—

When Sookie comes over to beg Lorelai to babysit her kids so she and Jackson can go on a quick ski retreat, she says that he loves to ski and she loves to curl up with a Sue Grafton mystery. If conditions are good,

Sookie says, she can "get a good eight hours of Kinsey Millhone in."

When Grafton released the first of her Alphabet Mystery Series in 1982, her coarse, no-nonsense female private eye, Kinsey Millhone, was groundbreaking—at the time, nearly all mystery writers and their lead detectives were male. From the way she hyped the getaway, Sookie has presumably read all seventeen preceding books in the bestselling series (starting with *A Is for Alibi* and continuing the "is for" convention through *Burglar*, *Corpse*, *Deadbeat*, *Evidence*, *Fugitive*, *Gumshoe*, *Homicide*, *Innocent*, *Judgment*, *Killer*, *Lawless*, *Malice*, *Noose*, *Outlaw*, *Peril*, and *Quarry*), and this world is a comfort read for her.

- *R Is for Ricochet* (2004) by Sue Grafton
- *S Is for Silence* (2005) by Sue Grafton

What books do you look forward to reading on lazy getaways? Is there a series, like this one, that you eagerly await new releases of?

> Unfortunately for Sookie—and all fans of the series—Sue Grafton died in 2017, just months after her twenty-fifth Millhone book, *Y Is for Yesterday*, was released. Grafton's daughter released a statement declaring that, because her mother would never have allowed a ghostwriter, "the alphabet now ends at Y."

Gender Trouble:
Feminism and
the Subversion of Identity

(1990) BY JUDITH BUTLER

Paris and Rory are taking a History of Feminism course together, and this book—a founding text of queer theory—is among those on the syllabus. In it, Butler separates gender from sex, furthering the idea that gender is a social construct that is socialized throughout our entire lives. What have you seen in your own life that could be regarded as gender socialization?

¿DÓNDE ESTÁ
LA BIBLIOTECA?

Isabel Allende is a Chilean American writer who has been called the world's most widely read Spanish-language author and the heir to Gabriel García Márquez's particular brand of magical realism. Rory mentions that *Eva Luna* is her favorite of Allende's twenty-plus novels, even though *The House of the Spirits* is a critically acclaimed favorite, as well as the book that put her on the literary map. Which

of these two books did you prefer? If you are bilingual, do you prefer to read books like these in Spanish? Do you think reading in the author's native language enhances the experience, or are translations able to convey the same story, even when they involve specific cultural phenomena, as Allende often does?

- *Eva Luna* (1987) by Isabel Allende
- *The House of the Spirits* (1982) by Isabel Allende

The Vanishing Newspaper
(2004) BY PHILIP MEYER

Mitchum suggests Rory read this book, which digs into the factors that made journalism, and particularly newspaper journalism, a viable business in the past, and how changing technologies were going to affect the industry. (Rory had already read it, natch.) In the book, Meyer predicts that, because of the changing digital landscape, newspapers will cease to exist as we currently know them—do you think that's a fair assessment? How often do you read daily newspapers, either in print or online? Do you subscribe to any local papers, or have those already disappeared in your area?

Love Medicine
(1984) BY LOUISE ERDRICH

How in the world did Luke end up with a daughter so similar to Rory? When April comes to stay with him for spring break, she brings a couple stacks of books and recites a rationalization that sounds very similar to Rory's season 2 reasons for traveling with bus, lunch, and just-in-case books. "I couldn't anticipate what I'd be in the mood for! Would I feel like reading Melville or McInerney? Or would I be in more of a Native-American-interconnected-short-narratives mood, in which case I'd go for the Louise Erdrich and some *Love Medicine*." *Love Medicine*, which won the 1984 National Book Critics Circle Award, weaves together the stories of five different families, each with varying internal and external problems. When you read books like this, do you think it's inevitable to see bits of your own family experience somewhere in the narrative? When you go on a trip, what kinds of books do you tend to pack or download ahead of time?

The Satanic Verses
(1988) BY SALMAN RUSHDIE

When Salman Rushdie based his novel in part on the life of the Islamic prophet Muhammad, he knew it would be controversial. Rushdie's title and backdrop came from the historic debate regarding satanic suggestion—the theory that the prophet Muhammad mistook some words about three pagan goddesses from Satan for being divine, so he included them in his sacred texts. But what was written to be a satiric meditation on identity, diaspora, and the social consequences of British colonialism in India was widely read as heretical and blasphemous. Ayatollah Khomeini issued a *fatwa* in 1989 calling for Rushdie and his publishers to be killed, and he needed twenty-four-hour police protection for a time. Assassination attempts have continued over the years, including one in 2022, when Rushdie was attacked onstage at a speaking engagement in Chautauqua, New York, during which he was repeatedly stabbed in the face and abdomen.

During an anxiety dream scene, a future Rory overhears Doyle saying that Salman Rushdie wants to come over for dinner, and a still-judgmental Paris is exasperated that he's such an important writer but his then-wife, Padma Lakshmi, just wanted to discuss cookbooks. When reading *The Satanic Verses*, was its satirical nature obvious to you or not? Do you understand why devout Muslims could be offended or outraged by this book? Regardless of your religion or personal beliefs, do you think books that satirize religion are difficult for people to read objectively?

Do you think the reaction to *The Satanic Verses* is similar to outrage over other works that poke at religious texts, such as José Saramago's *The Gospel According to Jesus Christ* (page 34; season 2, episode 3)? Why do you think satire is routinely misread?

Paradise Lost
(1667) BY JOHN MILTON

Rory worries that she tanked a final, even though she could have written about this epic poem all day. One of the primary themes of Milton's masterpiece is whether or not humans have free will or if their actions are predestined—it follows the events of the biblical Book of Genesis and the fall of man following the temptation of Adam and Eve in the Garden of Eden. Were you surprised by Milton's early portrayal of Satan as a complex and sympathetic character? Before reading *Paradise Lost*, what were your thoughts on free will? At the end of the work, do you believe Adam and Eve had free will? Why or why not?

The Unbearable Lightness of Being

(1984) BY MILAN KUNDERA

Kundera was set to be the commencement speaker at Rory's Yale graduation, to which Lorelai quipped that she was "unbearably light" on him, which isn't *exactly* what the book's title means. Kundera's novel explores the philosophical notion of weight—lightness and heaviness in relation to how one views life and their purpose in it, and, depending on your overall outlook, either lightness or heaviness could be fulfilling or an unbearable burden. Where do you think you fall on that scale, and would you wish to change that? Do you think it's possible to change something so innate to our beings?

RICHARD'S ESSENTIAL READS

Richard and Rory share a love of reading, and they quickly bonded over books by Mencken and Flaubert. But Richard also had his own specific taste in books, beyond his significant collection of Churchill biographies (see page 61). His leisure reads were as highbrow as he was—sweeping, multivolume histories; biographies of great thinkers and artists; and thoughtful collections of essays and poems.

A New History of the Peloponnesian War by Donald Kagan—four volumes (season 3, episode 10)

- *The Outbreak of the Peloponnesian War* (1969)
- *The Archidamian War* (1974)
- *The Peace of Nicias and the Sicilian Expedition* (1981)
- *The Fall of the Athenian Empire* (1987)

Richard loves a detailed accounting of major historical events, and this set was a sixtieth birthday gift from Lorelai (which was actually picked out by Rory). The Peloponnesian War, which spanned nearly thirty years in the fifth century BCE, pit Athens against Sparta for control over all the Greek lands. Did you study this war in school? If you were to pick a multivolume work about a historical conflict to read, which event would be your first choice?

Points of View (1958) by W. Somerset Maugham (season 4, episode 19)

Maugham spent decades as a popular playwright, with plays on both London and Broadway stages. But by the mid-1930s, he turned his attention solely to novels and short stories. This collection of five essays, which Richard was seen reading in his study, was released when he was eighty-four years old, some sixty-plus years after his first published work. Among the essays here are an appreciation for the works of the nineteenth-century multi-hyphenate Johann Goethe; a reflection on short stories, including those by Anton Chekhov; and a study on three French "journalists," by which he meant men who wrote journals that then became influential. Do you find essay collections like this interesting when they jump around between similar topics?

The History of the Decline and Fall of the Roman Empire (1776–1789) by Edward Gibbon (season 5, episode 5)

Richard said it took him thirty years to finish off this six-volume behemoth, but apparently a brief separation and some time alone in the pool house was all he needed to check it off his TBR list. It took Edward Gibbon, an English historian, nearly as long to research and write the volumes. Amazingly, when the first volume was released in 1776, it was immediately popular and Gibbon became a celebrity writer. If you had to devote roughly twenty-five years of your life to researching and writing on a single topic, what would it be?

Molloy (1955) by Samuel Beckett
(season 6, episode 5)

Much as Gibbon's history was on the decline of the Roman Empire, Beckett's most important nondramatic work was a lengthy dissertation on the decline of a man whose physical and mental facilities are failing him. Do you find it difficult to read works like this if you or someone close to you is also going through these health concerns? Do you think it could be comforting for someone like Richard—who had more natural health scares than anyone else on the show—to read about a character going through similarly difficult health problems?

Matisse the Master: A Life of Henri Matisse 1909–1954 (2005) by Hilary Spurling
(season 6, episode 7)

Matisse is considered one of the most important artists of the twentieth century, and his life was just as colorful as his paintings. This biography is actually the second volume of Spurling's extensive look at Matisse's life—the first, *The Unknown Matisse: A Life of Henri Matisse 1869–1908* (1998), covered his early years and his first success, up through the Fauvism era. This second biography covered the second half of his life, including spending time abroad, relocating to Nice, receiving divorce papers from his wife of forty years, living in occupied France during WWII, and his switch to creating art from paper cutouts, a necessity when he became wheelchair-bound and bedridden in his last years.

VOCAB: *Fauvism.* An artistic movement championed by Matisse that emphasized strong color over the more representative or realistic work of the Impressionists. Also referred to as "the Wild Beasts."

BONUS: Remember Darren quizzing Rory and the Springsteens about Fauvism after Lorelai complimented a Matisse-esque painting in his dining room?

Presuming Richard is now reading the second volume because he already finished the first, which portion of Matisse's life do you think he is most interested in? Matisse called his last decade, when he was physically restricted by health concerns, his *une seconde vie*, or second life—he created a whole new outlet for his creativity. When you reach this final stage of life, what do you want to be doing with your time? Do you think you will find new outlets for creativity, or find comfort in the creativity of others?

A Monetary History of the United States (1963) by Milton Friedman and Anna Jacobson Schwartz (season 7, episode 13)

After Richard's heart attack, Rory finds a bookmarked copy of this text by her grandpa's bed when she's searching his house for reading and listening materials. Richard had been teaching an economics course as a guest lecturer at Yale, and Rory was in the classroom when he fell to the ground. Of all the many items she brought to his hospital room, which included a record player, many albums, and a pile of nicely bound books, do you think Richard would want to keep rereading this in preparation for his lectures? What would you want your family to bring you if you were in his position?

Authors Referenced for Further Reading

Even with the numerous books read and referenced throughout *Gilmore Girls*, many more authors, journalists, and philosophers were name-checked without any specific book or writing being mentioned—not to mention that many of the living writers published work during the run of the series and long after the finale aired. They span the classic to the contemporary, and though we might not know which of their many works were being cited (except perhaps those by Marx or Machiavelli), we do know that adding a few more works to your TBR pile will bring you even closer to catching every little Roryism or Lorelaic line.

CHRISTIANE AMANPOUR
The Unfinished Revolution: Voices from the Global Fight for Women's Rights (2012)

Our Women on the Ground: Essays by Arab Women Reporting from the Arab World (2019)

R. W. APPLE JR.
Apple's America (2005)
Far Flung and Well Fed
 (2009)

HONORÉ DE BALZAC
Eugénie Grandet (1833)
Père Goriot (1835)

**ELIZABETH BARRETT
BROWNING**
"The Cry of the Children"
 (1842)
Sonnets from the Portuguese
 (1850)

JIMMY BRESLIN
*Can't Anybody Here Play This
 Game?* (1963)
The World According to Breslin
 (1984)

LORD BYRON
Childe Harold's Pilgrimage
 (1812–1818)
Don Juan (1819–1824)

MIGUEL DE CERVANTES
Don Quixote (1605)
*Los Trabajos de Persiles y
 Sigismunda* (1617)

NOAM CHOMSKY
*American Power and the New
 Mandarins* (1969)
Deterring Democracy (1991)

MICHAEL CRICHTON
The Andromeda Strain (1969)
Jurassic Park (1990)

PHILIP K. DICK
The Man in the High Castle
 (1962)
*Do Androids Dream of Electric
 Sheep?* (1968)

JOHN DOS PASSOS
Manhattan Transfer (1925)
The U.S.A. Trilogy
 • *The 42nd Parallel* (1930)
 • *1919* (1932)
 • *The Big Money* (1936)

MAUREEN DOWD
*Bushworld: Enter at Your Own
 Risk* (2004)
*The Year of Voting
 Dangerously: The
 Derangement of American
 Politics* (2016)

ARTHUR CONAN DOYLE
A Study in Scarlet (1887)
*The Adventures of Sherlock
   Holmes* (1892)

W. E. B. DU BOIS
The Souls of Black Folk (1903)
*Black Reconstruction in
   America* (1935)

EUCLID
The Elements (c. 300 BCE)
Optics (c. 300 BCE)

SUSAN FALUDI
*Backlash: The Undeclared
   War Against American
   Women* (1991)
*The Terror Dream: Fear
   and Fantasy in Post-9/11
   America* (2007)

ROBERT FROST
*Collected Poems of
   Robert Frost* (1930)
A Witness Tree (1942)

EUELL GIBBONS
*Stalking the Wild
   Asparagus* (1962)
*Stalking the Healthful
   Herbs* (1966)

C. Z. GUEST
First Garden (1987)
*Garden Talk: Ask Me
   Anything* (2001)

**CHRISTOPHER
ISHERWOOD**
Goodbye to Berlin (1939)
A Single Man (1964)

TAMA JANOWITZ
Slaves of New York (1986)
Area Code 212 (2002)

SØREN KIERKEGAARD
Fear and Trembling (1843)
The Essential Kierkegaard
   (1978)

FRAN LEBOWITZ
Metropolitan Life (1978)
The Fran Lebowitz Reader
   (1994)

JOHN LE CARRÉ
*The Spy Who Came in
   from the Cold* (1963)
Tinker, Tailor, Soldier, Spy
   (1974)

**NICCOLÒ
MACHIAVELLI**
Florentine Histories (1532)
The Prince (1532)

KARL MARX
The Communist Manifesto
   (1848)
Das Kapital (1867–1894)

JAY McINERNEY
Bright Lights, Big City (1984)
Story of My Life (1988)

JUDITH MILLER
One, by One, by One (1990)
God Has Ninety-Nine Names
   (1996)

JOSEPH MITCHELL
McSorley's Wonderful Saloon
   (1943)
*Up in the Old Hotel and Other
   Stories* (1992)

MOLIÈRE
Tartuffe (1664)
The Misanthrope (1666)

JOHN MUIR
Our National Parks (1901)
*My First Summer in the
   Sierra* (1911)

ROBERT MUSIL
The Man Without Qualities
   (1930–1943)
*Posthumous Papers of a Living
   Author* (1936)

ALEXANDER PUSHKIN
Eugene Onegin (1833)
The Bronze Horseman (1837)

HOWELL RAINES
*My Soul Is Rested: Movement
   Days in the Deep South
   Remembered* (1983)
The One that Got Away
   (2006)

GEORGE SAND
Indiana (1832)
La Mare au Diable (1846)

WILLIAM SAROYAN
The Time of Your Life (1939)
My Name is Aram (1940)

DR. SEUSS (THEODOR SEUSS GEISEL)
The Cat in the Hat (1957)
How the Grinch Stole Christmas! (1957)

ANNE SEXTON
Live or Die (1966)
The Death Notebooks (1974)

PATTI SMITH
Babel (1978)
Just Kids (2010)

GLORIA STEINEM
Outrageous Acts and Everyday Rebellions (1983)
Revolution from Within (1992)

NADINE STROSSEN
Defending Pornography: Free Speech, Sex, and the Fight for Women's Rights (1995)
Hate: Why We Should Resist It with Free Speech, Not Censorship (2018)

JONATHAN SWIFT
Gulliver's Travels (1726)
A Modest Proposal (1729)

HARRIET BEECHER STOWE
Uncle Tom's Cabin (1852)
The Minister's Wooing (1859)

IVAN TURGENEV
Fathers and Sons (1862)
Torrents of Spring (1872)

DAVID FOSTER WALLACE
Infinite Jest (1996)
Brief Interviews with Hideous Men (1999)

EDITH WHARTON
The House of Mirth (1905)
The Age of Innocence (1920)

OSCAR WILDE
The Picture of Dorian Gray (1890)
The Importance of Being Earnest (1895)

Book or Movie? Why Not Both?

The Gilmores love all forms of pop culture, and sometimes, it's hard to tell if they're referencing the book, the movie, or both. Sure, plenty of people can quote movie lines without having read the book, but based on the number of *Godfather* references Lorelai throws around, it's not absurd to think she might have read the groundbreaking book too.

So, consider this the ultimate read-and-watch twofer. When it comes to these popular movies and the often just-as-popular books they were based on, how often do you read or watch one and then go read or watch the other? Do you prefer to read the book first? And, the ultimate question—which was better, the book or the movie?

BOOK	MOVIE
Rosemary's Baby (1967) by Ira Levin	*Rosemary's Baby* (1968)
The Shining (1977) by Stephen King	*The Shining* (1980)
The Outsiders (1967) by S. E. Hinton	*The Outsiders* (1983)
The Godfather (1969) by Mario Puzo	The Godfather trilogy (1972–1990)
Cujo (1981) by Stephen King	*Cujo* (1983)
Rita Hayworth and Shawshank Redemption (1982) by Stephen King	The Shawshank Redemption (1994)
The Joy Luck Club (1989) by Amy Tan	*The Joy Luck Club* (1993)
The Lord of the Rings trilogy (1954–1955) by J. R. R. Tolkien	The Lord of the Rings trilogy (2001–2003)
Lisa and David (1961) by Dr. Theodore Isaac Rubin, M.D.	*David and Lisa* (1962)
The Final Days (1976) by Bob Woodward and Carl Bernstein	*The Final Days* (1989)
Whatever Happened to Baby Jane? (1960) by Henry Farrell	*Whatever Happened to Baby Jane?* (1962)
Girl, Interrupted (1993) by Susanna Kaysen	*Girl, Interrupted* (1999)
Reversal of Fortune (1985) by Alan Dershowitz	*Reversal of Fortune* (1990)
Shane (1949) by Jack Schaefer	*Shane* (1953)
Marathon Man (1974) by William Goldman	*Marathon Man* (1976)
Fast Times at Ridgemont High (1981) by Cameron Crowe	*Fast Times at Ridgemont High* (1982)
The Wonderful Wizard of Oz (1900) by L. Frank Baum	*The Wizard of Oz* (1939)

BOOK	MOVIE
How the Grinch Stole Christmas! (1957) by Dr. Seuss	*How the Grinch Stole Christmas!* (1966)
Stuart Little (1945) by E. B. White	*Stuart Little* (1999)
Babe the Gallant Pig (1983) by Dick King-Smith	*Babe* (1995)
Gidget (1957) by Frederick Kohner	*Gidget* (1959)
Mutiny on the Bounty by Charles Nordhoff and James Norman Hall (1932)	*Mutiny on the Bounty* (1935)
The Stepford Wives (1972) by Ira Levin	*The Stepford Wives* (1975)
The Adventures of Pinocchio (1883) by Carlo Collodi	*Pinocchio* (1940)
The Witches of Eastwick (1984) by John Updike	*The Witches of Eastwick* (1987)
Dracula (1897) by Bram Stoker	*Dracula* (1931)
Being There (1971) by Jerzy Kosinski	*Being There* (1979)
A Beautiful Mind (1998) by Sylvia Nassar	*A Beautiful Mind* (2001)

Keep Reading
with Rory

A POST-2007 SUPPLEMENTAL LIST

In the years that have passed since *Gilmore Girls* went off the air, so many amazing books have been released that Rory would have certainly put on her "to buy" pile if she were working at Stars Hollow Books. And because Rory was always good about mixing contemporary releases with old classics, we threw in a few that seem like the kind she would have added to her shelves eventually.

This supplemental reading list is an attempt to diversify the authors and stories told, broaden horizons and lines of thinking, and overall expose readers to a wider range of experiences than standard curricula tends to.

All these selections stay within the realm of literature Rory would appreciate, though! There are thorough histories, literary bestsellers, and award winners. There are novels that read as poetry and newly released works by her favorite long-dead authors. There are collections of essays and deep dives into journalism. And of course, there are some pop culture desserts thrown in for good measure.

- *Americanah* (2013) by Chimamanda Ngozi Adichie
- *My Way: An Autobiography* (2013) by Paul Anka
  With a family pet named for the Canadian teen idol, Anka's autobiography would surely end up in Rory's Amazon cart—if not for her, then as a gift for Lorelai.

- *A Handmaid's Tale* (1985) by Margaret Atwood
- *Notes of a Native Son* (1955) by James Baldwin
- *Fun Home: A Family Tragicomic* (2006) by Alison Bechdel
- *Midnight in the Garden of Good and Evil* (1994) by John Berendt
- *The Yellow House* (2019) by Sarah M. Broom
- *Parable of the Sower* (1993) by Octavia E. Butler
- *Alexander Hamilton* (2004) by Ron Chernow
  This bestselling biography has everything: a hero overcoming improbable odds; a who's who of Founding Fathers (and their dirt); the creation of a new system of government; and the nation's first sex scandal. And, of course, an eventual Tony-winning musical that became an instant classic.

- *All You Can Ever Know* (2018) by Nicole Chung
- *Between the World and Me* (2015) by Ta-Nehisi Coates

- ***Bad Feminist*** (2014) by Roxane Gay
  Rory loves a collection of essays, and this one, by cultural critic and professor Roxane Gay, speaks directly to another of her loves: pop culture.

- ***Homegoing*** (2016) by Yaa Gyasi
  An exquisite and stirring novel, Homegoing *follows the multi-generational trauma and fallout of two lineages divided by the transatlantic slave trade.*

- ***The 1619 Project: A New Origin Story*** (2019) by Nikole Hannah-Jones

- ***The Other Black Girl*** (2021) by Zakiya Dalila Harris

- ***She Said: Breaking the Sexual Harassment Story That Helped Ignite a Movement*** (2019) by Jodi Kantor and Megan Twohey
  The inside account of how two female journalists broke one of the biggest stories of the decade. A must-read for any journalist, investigative or not.

- ***A Natural Woman: A Memoir*** (2012) by Carole King

- ***On Writing: A Memoir of the Craft*** (2000) by Stephen King

- ***Interpreter of Maladies*** (1999) by Jhumpa Lahiri

- ***Devil in the White City*** (2003) by Erik Larson

- ***Pachinko*** (2017) by Min Jin Lee

- ***Her Body and Other Parties*** (2017) by Carmen Maria Machado

- ***Wolf Hall*** (2009) by Hilary Mantel

  The first book in Mantel's heavily researched, award-winning trilogy of Thomas Cromwell novels (Bring Up the Bodies [2012] and The Mirror and the Light [2020] round out the set), this seems like just the sort of series that Rory and Richard could have long discussions over after a Friday night dinner.

- ***The Song of Achilles*** (2011) by Madeline Miller
- ***Beloved*** (1987) by Toni Morrison
- ***The Audacity of Hope*** (2006) by Barack Obama

  As we know from the final episode of the series, Rory is off to cover her first presidential campaign—and wow did she luck out in that department! Trailing the young senator from Illinois, Barack Obama, this could be a career-making experience for her, and any journalist worth her press pass would be sure to read everything by and about the candidate they're covering.

- ***When the Emperor was Divine*** (2002) by Julie Otsuka
- ***Songteller: My Life in Lyrics*** (2020) by Dolly Parton

  Dolly Parton got a couple of mentions over the course of the series—namely when Lorelai and Rory return from Atlantic City and tease Luke that a Dolly impersonator was his double, and when Lorelai sang her Dolly-inspired rendition of "I Will Always Love You" at karaoke. But the music legend's detailed accounts of the inspiration behind her songs, the stories of her life, and the history of her sixty-plus years in the industry could serve as banter fodder for years.

- ***Essential Essays: Culture, Politics, and the Art of Poetry*** (2018) by Adrienne Rich
- ***The Immortal Life of Henrietta Lacks*** (2011) by Rebecca Skloot
- ***White Teeth*** (2000) by Zadie Smith
- ***A Gentleman in Moscow*** (2016) by Amor Towles
  Considering Rory's love of all things classical Russian, this novel about a count living out his permanent house arrest in a luxury Moscow hotel during the Stalin era would be right up her alley.

- ***The Autobiography of Mark Twain*** (2010–2015) edited by the Mark Twain Project
  Exactly one hundred years after his death, as per his wishes, the full volumes of Mark Twain's autobiography were finally released. We imagine Rory would have been first in line to snag a copy.

- ***On Earth We're Briefly Gorgeous*** (2019) by Ocean Vuong
- ***The Underground Railroad*** (2016) by Colson Whitehead
- ***Solito*** (2022) by Javier Zamora

Suggested Reads

Thjs supplemental book index isn't part of the *Gilmore Girls* canon, but it includes all of the "Keep Reading with Rory" updated suggestions, as well as others mentioned throughout this book, such as Richard's possible Churchill shelf finds and examples used in the various essays. Follow the legend if you're looking for a specific genre or type of book—perhaps you're in the mood for a poetry book (P), or a narrative nonfiction (NNF).

LEGEND BY BOOK TYPE

F—Fiction

NF—Nonfiction

NNF—Narrative Nonfiction

B—Biography

M—Memoir or
   Autobiography

P—Poetry

E—Essays

SS—Short Stories

COL—Collection

T—Play/Theater

TB—Textbook

SH—Self-Help

RT—Religious Text

REF—Reference Book

- ☐ Achebe, Chinua; ***Things Fall Apart*** (1958) **F**
- ☐ Adichie, Chimamanda Ngozi; ***Americanah*** (2013) **F**
- ☐ Atwood, Margaret; ***A Handmaid's Tale*** (1985) **F**
- ☐ Austen, Jane; ***Emma*** (1815) **F**
- ☐ Austen, Jane; ***Pride and Prejudice*** (1813) **F**
- ☐ Austen, Jane; ***Sense and Sensibility*** (1811) **F**
- ☐ Baldwin, James; ***Notes of a Native Son*** (1955) **E**
- ☐ Bechdel, Alison; ***Fun Home: A Family Tragicomic*** (2006) **M**
- ☐ Berendt, John; ***Midnight in the Garden of Good and Evil*** (1994) **NNF**
- ☐ Broom, Sarah M.; ***The Yellow House*** (2019) **M**
- ☐ Brontë, Charlotte; ***Jane Eyre*** (1847) **F**
- ☐ Brontë, Charlotte; ***Shirley*** (1849) **F**
- ☐ Brontë, Charlotte; ***Villette*** (1853) **F**
- ☐ Bushnell, Candace; ***Sex and the City*** (1996) **M**
- ☐ Butler, Octavia E.; ***Parable of the Sower*** (1993) **F**
- ☐ Chernow, Ron; ***Alexander Hamilton*** (2004) **B**
- ☐ Chung, Nicole; ***All You Can Ever Know*** (2018) **M**
- ☐ Churchill, Winston; ***My Early Life*** (1930) **M**
- ☐ Churchill, Winston; ***The Second World War*** (1948–1953) **NF**
  - ☐ ***The Gathering Storm*** (1948) **NF**
  - ☐ ***Their Finest Hour*** (1949) **NF**
  - ☐ ***The Grand Alliance*** (1950) **NF**
  - ☐ ***The Hinge of Fate*** (1950) **NF**
  - ☐ ***Closing the Ring*** (1951) **NF**
  - ☐ ***Triumph and Tragedy*** (1953) **NF**
- ☐ Coates, Ta-Nehisi; ***Between the World and Me*** (2015) **NNF**
- ☐ Colette; ***Claudine at School*** (1900) **F**
- ☐ Colette; ***Claudine in Paris*** (1901) **F**

☐ Colette; ***Claudine Married*** (1902) **F**

☐ Colette; ***Claudine and Anne*** (1903) **F**

☐ Cook, Blanche Wiesen; ***Eleanor Roosevelt: Volume 2, The Defining Years, 1933–1938*** (2000) **B**

☐ Cook, Blanche Wiesen; ***Eleanor Roosevelt: Volume 3, The War Years and After, 1939–1962*** (2016) **B**

☐ Faulkner, William; ***Absalom, Absalom!*** (1936) **F**

☐ Faulkner, William; ***As I Lay Dying*** (1930) **F**

☐ Faulkner, William; ***Flags in the Dust*** (1973) **F**

☐ Faulkner, William; ***Go Down, Moses*** (1942) **F**

☐ Faulkner, William; ***The Hamlet*** (1940) **F**

☐ Faulkner, William; ***Intruder in the Dust*** (1948) **F**

☐ Faulkner, William; ***Light in August*** (1932) **F**

☐ Faulkner, William; ***The Mansion*** (1959) **F**

☐ Faulkner, William; ***The Reivers*** (1962) **F**

☐ Faulkner, William; ***Requiem for a Nun*** (1951) **F**

☐ Faulkner, William; ***Sanctuary*** (1931) **F**

☐ Faulkner, William; ***Sartoris*** (1929) **F**

☐ Faulkner, William; ***The Town*** (1957) **F**

☐ Faulkner, William; ***The Unvanquished*** (1938) **F**

☐ Gardiner, Muriel; ***Code Name Mary*** (1983) **M**

☐ Gay, Roxane; ***Bad Feminist*** (2014) **E**

☐ Gilbert, Martin; ***Churchill: A Life*** (1991) **B**

☐ Grafton, Sue; **Alphabet Mystery series** (25 books) (1982–2017) **F**

☐ Gregory, Philippa; ***The Kingmaker's Daughter*** (2012) **F**

☐ Gyasi, Yaa; ***Homegoing*** (2016) **F**

☐ Hannah-Jones, Nikole; ***The 1619 Project: A New Origin Story*** (2019) **NF**

☐ Harris, Zakiya Dalila; ***The Other Black Girl*** (2021) **F**

☐ Hellman, Lillian; ***Pentimento*** (1973) **F**

☐ Holt, Jim; *Stop Me If You've Heard This: A History and Philosophy of Jokes* (2008) **E**

☐ Joyce, James; **Ulysses** (1922) **F**

☐ Kantor, Jodi, and Megan Twohey; *She Said: Breaking the Sexual Harassment Story That Helped Ignite a Movement* (2019) **NF**

☐ King, Carole; *A Natural Woman: A Memoir* (2012) **M**

☐ King, Stephen; *On Writing: A Memoir of the Craft* (2000) **M**

☐ Lahiri, Jhumpa; *Interpreter of Maladies* (1999) **SS**

☐ Larson, Erik; *Devil in the White City* (2003) **NNF**

☐ Lee, Min Jin; *Pachinko* (2017) **F**

☐ Machado, Carmen Maria; *Her Body and Other Parties* (2017) **SS**

☐ Mantel, Hilary; *Wolf Hall* (2009) **F**

☐ Mantel, Hilary; *Bring Up the Bodies* (2012) **F**

☐ Mantel, Hilary; *The Mirror and the Light* (2020) **F**

☐ Miller, Madeline; *The Song of Achilles* (2011) **F**

☐ Montgomery, Lucy Maud; *Anne of Green Gables* (1908) **F**

☐ Moreno-Garcia, Silvia; *Mexican Gothic* (2020) **F**

☐ Morrison, Toni; *Beloved* (1987) **F**

☐ Obama, Barack; *The Audacity of Hope* (2006) **NF**

☐ Otsuka, Julie; *When the Emperor was Divine* (2002) **F**

☐ Parton, Dolly; *Songteller: My Life in Lyrics* (2020) **M**

☐ Pollard, A. J.; *Warwick the Kingmaker* (2007) **B**

☐ Reynolds, David; *In Command of History: Churchill Fighting and Writing the Second World War* (2005) **B**

☐ Rich, Adrienne; *Essential Essays: Culture, Politics, and the Art of Poetry* (2018) **E**

☐ Roberts, Andrew; *Churchill: Walking with Destiny* (2018) **B**

☐ Sandys, Celia; *Churchill: Wanted Dead or Alive* (2019) **B**

- ☐ Skloot, Rebecca; *The Immortal Life of Henrietta Lacks* (2011) **NF**
- ☐ Smith, Zadie; *White Teeth* (2000) **F**
- ☐ Spurling, Hilary; *The Unknown Matisse: A Life of Henri Matisse 1869–1908* (1998) **B**
- ☐ Stine, R. L.; **Goosebumps series** (62 books) (1992–1997) **F**
- ☐ Symonds, John Addington; *Studies of the Greek Poets* (1873) **NF**
- ☐ Thompson, Hunter S.; *Hell's Angels: The Strange and Terrible Saga of the Outlaw Motorcycle Gangs* (1967) **NF**
- ☐ Thompson, Hunter S.; *The Rum Diary* (1998) **F**
- ☐ Towles, Amor; *A Gentleman in Moscow* (2016) **F**
- ☐ Tucker-Jones, Anthony; *Churchill, Master and Commander: Winston Churchill at War 1895–1945* (2021) **B**
- ☐ Twain, Mark; *The Autobiography of Mark Twain* (3 volumes) (2010–2015) **M**
- ☐ Vuong, Ocean; *On Earth We're Briefly Gorgeous* (2019) **F**
- ☐ Walker, Alice; *The Color Purple* (1982) **F**
- ☐ Whitehead; Colson; *The Underground Railroad* (2016) **F**
- ☐ Wolfe, Tom; *Bonfire of the Vanities* (1987) **F**
- ☐ Wright, Betty Ren; *The Dollhouse Murders* (1983) **F**
- ☐ Zamora, Javier; *Solito* (2022) **M**

Episode Guide Index

L ooking for a specific read? Or just want to see how many books you've been able to check off your list? You've come to the right place. In addition to listing each book by its author and publication date, this index also includes the episode reference number (4.17, for example, means season 4, episode 17). See page 226 for the legend to genre, type of book, etc.

☐ Baum, Vicki; *Hotel Berlin '43* (1944) (3.14) **F**

☐ Beckett, Samuel; *Molloy* (1955) (6.5) **F**

☐ Beckett, Samuel; *Waiting for Godot* (1953) (2.18) **T**

☐ Behrendt, Greg, and Liz Tuccillo;
He's Just Not That Into You (2004) (5.17) **F**

☐ *The Bhagavad Gita* (1st millennium BCE) (2.18) **RT**

☐ *The Bible* (c. 1450s) (3.20) **RT**

☐ Binyon, T. J.; *Pushkin: A Biography* (2002) (5.16) **B**

☐ Blume, Judy; *Deenie* (1973) (3.6) **F**

☐ Blyth, R. H.; *Haiku, Volume 2: Spring* (1981) (4.3) **P**

☐ Bolles, Richard Nelson; *What Color Is Your Parachute?*
(2001) (2.21) **SH**

☐ Bourdain, Anthony; *Kitchen Confidential: Adventures in
the Culinary Underbelly* (2000) (1.4) **NF**

☐ Bridwell, Norman; *Clifford the Big Red Dog* (1963) (5.17) **F**

☐ Brontë, Emily; *Wuthering Heights* (1847) (4.10) **F**

☐ Brown, Dale; *Fatal Terrain* (1997) (3.14) **F**

☐ Brown, Dan; *The Da Vinci Code* (2003) (5.2) **F**

☐ Bukowski, Charles; *Notes of a Dirty Old Man*
(1969) (2.15) **NF**

☐ Burroughs, William S.; *Naked Lunch* (1959) (3.21) **F**

☐ Butler, Judith; *Gender Trouble: Feminism and the
Subversion of Identity* (1990) (7.14) **NF**

☐ Capote, Truman; *In Cold Blood* (1965) (7.1) **NNF**

☐ Carroll, Lewis; *Alice's Adventures in Wonderland*
(1865) (4.16) **F**

☐ Clinton, Hillary; *It Takes a Village* (1996) (6.11) **NF**

☐ Collins, Billy; *Sailing Alone Around the Room: New and
Selected Poems* (2001) (6.16) **P**

☐ *The Compact Oxford English Dictionary* (1991) (2.6) **REF**

- [ ] Congreve, William; *The Mourning Bride* (1697) (2.9) **T**
- [ ] Conrad, Joseph; *Lord Jim* (1900) (3.14) **F**
- [ ] Cook, Blanche Wiesen; *Eleanor Roosevelt: Volume 1, 1884–1933* (1992) (3.20) **B**
- [ ] Crane, Stephen; *The Red Badge of Courage* (1895) (6.20) **F**
- [ ] Davies, Robertson; *The Manticore* (1972) (3.3) **F**
- [ ] de Beauvoir, Simone; *Memoirs of a Dutiful Daughter* (1958) (2.7) **M**
- [ ] Des Barres, Pamela; *I'm with the Band: Confessions of a Groupie* (1987) (3.16) **M**
- [ ] Dickens, Charles; *A Christmas Carol* (1843) (3.7) **F**
- [ ] Dickens, Charles; *A Tale of Two Cities* (1859) (1.2) **F**
- [ ] Dickens, Charles; *David Copperfield* (1850) (1.2) **F**
- [ ] Dickens, Charles; *Great Expectations* (1861) (1.2) **F**
- [ ] Dickens, Charles; *Little Dorrit* (1857) (1.2) **F**
- [ ] Dickens, Charles; *Nicholas Nickleby* (1839) (3.17) **F**
- [ ] Dickens, Charles; *Oliver Twist* (1838) (2.5) **F**
- [ ] Dickinson, Emily; *The Poems of Emily Dickinson* (1955) (1.11) **P**
- [ ] Didion, Joan; *The Year of Magical Thinking* (2005) (6.15) **M**
- [ ] Dinesen, Isak; *Out of Africa* (1937) (1.20) **M**
- [ ] Dostoevsky, Fyodor; *The Brothers Karamazov* (1880) (2.5) **F**
- [ ] Dostoevsky, Fyodor; *Demons* (1872) (5.16) **F**
- [ ] Dunn, Sarah; *The Big Love* (2004) (6.13) **F**
- [ ] Eggers, Dave; *A Heartbreaking Work of Staggering Genius* (2000) (5.15) **M**
- [ ] Ehrenreich, Barbara; *Nickel and Dimed: On (Not) Getting By in America* (2001) (3.13) **NF**
- [ ] Erdrich, Louise; *Love Medicine* (1984) (7.17) **F**

☐ Esquivel, Laura; *Like Water for Chocolate* (1989) (2.15) **F**

☐ Faber, Michel; *The Crimson Petal and the White* (2002) (4.16) **F**

☐ Faulkner, William; *The Sound and the Fury* (1929) (2.7) **F**

☐ Fisher, M. F. K.; *The Art of Eating* (1954) (1.17) **F**

☐ Fitzgerald, F. Scott; *The Great Gatsby* (1925) (3.11) **F**

☐ Fitzgerald, F. Scott; *Tender is the Night* (1934) (4.5) **F**

☐ Flaubert, Gustave; *Madame Bovary* (1857) (1.1) **F**

☐ Fodor's; *Selected Hotels of Europe* (1987) (3.13) **REF**

☐ Fonda, Jane; *My Life So Far* (2005) (7.1) **M**

☐ Foulkes, Christopher; *Larousse Encyclopedia of Wine* (1994) (5.20) **REF**

☐ Franken, Al; *Lies and the Lying Liars Who Tell Them* (2003) (4.13) **NF**

☐ Friedman, Milton, and Anna Jacobson Schwartz; *A Monetary History of the United States* (1963) (7.13) **NF**

☐ Gibbon, Edward; *The History of the Decline and Fall of the Roman Empire* (1776–1789) (5.5) **NF**

☐ Gibson, William; *The Miracle Worker* (1959) (1.10) **T**

☐ Gilbert, Stuart; *James Joyce's Ulysses: A Study* (1930) (1.20) **NF**

☐ Ginsburg, Allen; *Howl and Other Poems* (1956) (2.5) **P**

☐ Gogol, Nikolai Vasilyevich; *Dead Souls* (1842) (3.3) **F**

☐ *Golden Book Illustrated Encyclopedias* (1988) (1.16) **REF**

☐ Grafton, Sue; *R is for Ricochet* (2004) (7.11) **F**

☐ Grafton, Sue; *S is for Silence* (2005) (7.11) **F**

☐ Grimm, Wilhelm and Jacob (the Brothers Grimm); **"Snow-White and Rose-Red"** (1812) (2.7) **F**

☐ Haddon, Mark; *The Curious Incident of the Dog in the Night-time* (2003) (5.6) **F**

☐ Hathaway, Katharine Butler; *The Little Locksmith* (1943) (2.20) **M**

☐ Hawthorne, Nathaniel; *The Scarlet Letter* (1850) (5.11) **F**

☐ Heaney, Seamus; *Beowulf: A New Verse Translation* (1999) (6.10) **P**

☐ Heinl, Robert Debs and Nancy Gordon Heinl; *Written in Blood: The Story of the Haitian People 1492–1995* (1996) (5.20) **NF**

☐ Hellman, Lillian; *The Children's Hour* (1934) **T**

☐ Hemingway, Ernest; *The Old Man and the Sea* (1952) (4.11) **F**

☐ Hemingway, Ernest; **"The Snows of Kilimanjaro"** (1936) (4.6) **SS**

☐ Hemingway, Ernest; *The Sun Also Rises* (1926) **F**

☐ Hersh, Seymour M.; *My Lai 4: A Report on the Massacre and Its Aftermath* (1970) (5.12) **NF**

☐ Homer; *The Iliad* (8th century BCE) (5.7) **P**

☐ Homer; *The Odyssey* (8th century BCE) (5.7) **P**

☐ Hornby, Nick; *High Fidelity* (1995) (2.21) **F**

☐ Houseman, John; *Unfinished Business: Memoirs 1902–1988* (2000) (2.9) **M**

☐ Hugo, Victor; *The Hunchback of Notre-Dame* (1831) (1.2) **F**

☐ Hume, David; *An Enquiry Concerning the Principles of Morals* (1751) (5.11) **NF**

☐ Iacocca, Lee, with William Novak; *Iacocca: An Autobiography* (1984) (3.16) **M**

☐ Irvin, Jim; *The Mojo Collection: The Ultimate Music Companion* (2001) (2.5) **NF**

☐ Jackson, Shirley; **"The Lottery"** (1948) (2.21) **SS**

☐ James, Henry; **"The Art of Fiction"** (1884) (1.20) **E**

- [ ] James, Henry; *Daisy Miller* (1879) (5.1) **F**
- [ ] Johnson, Crockett; *Harold and the Purple Crayon* (1955) (6.20) **F**
- [ ] Johnson, Spencer; *Who Moved My Cheese?* (1998) (2.4) **SH**
- [ ] Kafka, Franz; *The Metamorphosis* (1915) (1.10) **F**
- [ ] Kafka, Franz; *The Trial* (1925) (4.19) **F**
- [ ] Kagan, Donald; *A New History of the Peloponnesian War* (3.10) (4 volumes) **NF**
  - [ ] *The Outbreak of the Peloponnesian War* (1969) **NF**
  - [ ] *The Archidamian War* (1974) **NF**
  - [ ] *The Peace of Nicias and the Sicilian Expedition* (1981) **NF**
  - [ ] *The Fall of the Athenian Empire* (1987) **NF**
- [ ] Keene, Carolyn; **The Nancy Drew series** (56 books) (1930–1979) (5.12) **F**
- [ ] Keene, Carolyn; **Nancy Drew 33:** *The Witch Tree Symbol* (1955) (1.17) **F**
- [ ] Kennedy, William; *Ironweed* (1983) (7.8) **F**
- [ ] Kerouac, Jack; *On the Road* (1957) (2.5) **F**
- [ ] Kerouac, Jack; *Visions of Cody* (1972) (3.5) **F**
- [ ] King, Stephen; *Carrie* (1974) (1.13) **F**
- [ ] Klein, Joe; *Primary Colors* (1996) (6.9) **F**
- [ ] Kundera, Milan; *The Unbearable Lightness of Being* (1984) (7.21) **F**
- [ ] Kushner, Tony; *Angels in America* (1991) (5.17) **T**
- [ ] *Larousse Gastronomique*; 2001 English edition, edited by Prosper Montagné (4.16) **REF**
- [ ] Lawrence, Jerome, and Robert E. Lee; *Inherit the Wind* (1955) (2.15) **T**
- [ ] Lee, Harper; *To Kill a Mockingbird* (1960) (2.8) **F**
- [ ] Lewis, C. S.; *The Lion, the Witch and the Wardrobe* (1950) (6.4) **F**

- [ ] Lewis, Sinclair; *Elmer Gantry* (1927) (2.3) **F**
- [ ] Lipton, Lawrence; *The Holy Barbarians* (1959) (3.14) **NF**
- [ ] Lofting, Hugh; *The Story of Doctor Dolittle* (1920) (2.18) **F**
- [ ] Lovell, Mary S.; *The Sisters: The Saga of the Mitford Family* (2002) (6.13) **B**
- [ ] Macaulay, David; *The New Way Things Work* (1998) (6.20) **NF**
- [ ] MacNeil, Karen; *The Wine Bible* (2000) (5.20) **REF**
- [ ] Mailer, Norman; *The Armies of the Night: History as a Novel, the Novel as History* (1968) (5.6) **NF**
- [ ] Mailer, Norman; *The Executioner's Song* (1979) (5.6) **F**
- [ ] Mailer, Norman; *The Naked and the Dead* (1948) (5.6) **F**
- [ ] Maleska, Eugene T.; *The New York Times Daily Crossword Puzzles, Volume 36* (1994) (2.19)
- [ ] Mamet, David; *Glengarry Glen Ross* (1983) (1.18) **T**
- [ ] Mann, Thomas; *The Magic Mountain* (1924) (3.7) **F**
- [ ] Márquez, Gabriel García; *One Hundred Years of Solitude* (1967) (3.20) **F**
- [ ] Martha Stewart Living; *The Best of Martha Stewart Living: Holidays* (1993) (6.10) **REF**
- [ ] Maugham, W. Somerset; *Points of View* (1958) (4.19) **E**
- [ ] McCarthy, Cormac; *All the Pretty Horses* (1992) (6.14) **F**
- [ ] McCarthy, Mary; *A Bolt from the Blue and Other Essays* (2002) (3.1) **E**
- [ ] McCarthy, Mary; *The Group* (1963) (1.9) **F**
- [ ] McCourt, Frank; *Angela's Ashes* (1996) (6.11) **M**
- [ ] McEwan, Ian; *Atonement* (2001) (4.3) **F**
- [ ] McNeil, Legs, and Gillian McCain; *Please Kill Me: The Uncensored Oral History of Punk* (1996) (2.19) **NF**
- [ ] Melville, Herman; *Billy Budd and Other Tales* (1924) (4.12) **F**

- [ ] Melville, Herman; *Moby-Dick; or, The Whale* (1851) (1.1) **F**
- [ ] Mencken, H. L.; *A Mencken Chrestomathy* (1948) (1.3) **COL**
- [ ] Mencken, H. L.; *The Days* [3 volumes] (1947) (1.3) **M**
- [ ] Metalious, Grace; *Peyton Place* (1956) (1.3) **F**
- [ ] Meyer, Philip; *The Vanishing Newspaper* (2004) (7.15) **NF**
- [ ] Milford, Nancy; *Savage Beauty: The Life of Edna St. Vincent Millay* (2001) (2.7) **B**
- [ ] Miller, Arthur; *The Crucible* (1953) (1.7) **T**
- [ ] Miller, Henry; *Sexus* (1949) (7.3) **F**
- [ ] Milton, John; *Paradise Lost* (1667) (7.20) **P**
- [ ] Mitchell, Margaret; *Gone With the Wind* (1936) (1.16) **F**
- [ ] Mitford, Nancy; *The Pursuit of Love* (1945) (5.3) **F**
- [ ] Mitford, Nancy; *Love in a Cold Climate* (1949) (5.3) **F**
- [ ] Montefiore, Simon Sebag; *Stalin: The Court of the Red Tsar* (2003) (6.22) **B**
- [ ] Moore, Barrington, Jr.; *Social Origins of Dictatorship and Democracy: Lord and Peasant in the Making of the Modern World* (1966) (5.17) **NF**
- [ ] Mötley Crüe and Neil Strauss; *The Dirt: Confessions of the World's Most Notorious Rock Band* (2001) (2.18) **M**
- [ ] Murkoff, Heidi; *What to Expect When You're Expecting* (1984) (7.3) **REF**
- [ ] Nietzsche, Friedrich; *The Portable Nietzsche* (1954) (2.21) **COL**
- [ ] *The Norton Anthologies* (7.9) **COL**
- [ ] *Norton Critical Edition Reference Books* (3.5) **REF**
- [ ] O'Connor, Evangeline; *Who's Who and What's What in Shakespeare* (1987) (1.4) **REF**
- [ ] Orwell, George; *Nineteen Eighty-Four* (1949) (4.7) **F**
- [ ] Pagels, Elaine; *The Gnostic Gospels* (1979) (4.13) **NF**

☐ Parker, Dorothy; *The Portable Dorothy Parker* (1944) (1.9) **COL**

☐ Plath, Sylvia; *The Bell Jar* (1963) (3.3) **F**

☐ Plath, Sylvia; *The Unabridged Journals of Sylvia Plath* (2000) (1.12) **M**

☐ Poe, Edgar Allan; **"The Cask of Amontillado"** (1846) (3.17) **SS**

☐ Poe, Edgar Allan; **"The Raven"** (1845) (3.17) **SS**

☐ Poe, Edgar Allan; **"The System of Doctor Tarr and Professor Fether"** (1845) (3.17) **SS**

☐ Poe, Edgar Allan; **"The Tell-Tale Heart"** (1843) (3.17) **SS**

☐ Powell, Dawn; *Novels: 1930–1962* (2 volumes) (2.20) **F**

☐ Powell, Dawn; *Selected Letters of Dawn Powell (1913–1965)* (1999) (2.5) **COL**

☐ Powell, William; *The Anarchist Cookbook* (1971) (5.6) **F**

☐ Proust, Marcel; *In Search of Lost Time* (1927) (3.17) **F**

☐ Proust, Marcel; *Swann's Way* (1913) (1.11) **F**

☐ Rand, Ayn; *The Fountainhead* (1943) (2.13) **F**

☐ Rand, Ayn; *Letters of Ayn Rand* (1995) (edited by Michael S. Berliner) (3.5) **COL**

☐ Rilke, Rainer Maria; *Letters to a Young Poet* (1929) (2.15) **COL**

☐ Robert, Henry; *Robert's Rules of Order* (1876) (6.14) **REF**

☐ Ronay, Egon; *Hotels, Restaurants and Inns of Great Britain and Ireland* (1986) (3.13) **REF**

☐ Rough Guides; *The Rough Guide to Europe on a Budget* (2003) (3.13) **REF**

☐ Rowling, J. K.; *Harry Potter and the Sorcerer's Stone* (1997) (6.20) **F**

☐ Rowling, J. K.; *Harry Potter and the Chamber of Secrets* (1998) (6.20) **F**

- [ ] Rowling, J. K.; *Harry Potter and the Prisoner of Azkaban* (1999) (6.20) **F**
- [ ] Rowling, J. K.; *Harry Potter and the Goblet of Fire* (2000) (6.20) **F**
- [ ] Rowling, J. K.; *Harry Potter and the Order of the Phoenix* (2003) (6.20) **F**
- [ ] Rowling, J. K.; *Harry Potter and the Half-Blood Prince* (2005) (6.20) **F**
- [ ] Rowling, J. K.; *Harry Potter and the Deathly Hallows* (2007) (6.20) **F**
- [ ] Rushdie, Salman; *The Satanic Verses* (1988) (7.20) **F**
- [ ] Sagan, Carl; *Contact* (1985) (2.12) **F**
- [ ] Salinger, J. D.; *Franny and Zooey* (1961) (2.15) **F**
- [ ] Salinger, J. D.; *The Catcher in the Rye* (1951) (2.8) **F**
- [ ] Saramago, José; *The Gospel According to Jesus Christ* (1991) (2.3) **F**
- [ ] Sebold, Alice; *The Lovely Bones* (2002) (3.21) **F**
- [ ] Seneca, Lucius Annaeus; *Letters from a Stoic* (c. 65 CE) (2.4) **COL**
- [ ] Shakespeare, William; *The Comedy of Errors* (c. 1590s) (1.4) **T**
- [ ] Shakespeare, William; *Hamlet* (c. 1600) (1.18) **T**
- [ ] Shakespeare, William; *Henry IV* parts 1 and 2 (c. 1597) (3.3) **T**
- [ ] Shakespeare, William; *Henry V* (1599) (3.3) **T**
- [ ] Shakespeare, William; *Henry VI* (c. 1592) (3.20) **T**
- [ ] Shakespeare, William; *Julius Caesar* (c. 1599) (3.11) **T**
- [ ] Shakespeare, William; *Macbeth* (c. 1606) (3.3) **T**
- [ ] Shakespeare, William; *The Merry Wives of Windsor* (1602) (3.3) **T**

- [ ] Shakespeare, William; ***Othello*** (1603) (2.19) **T**
- [ ] Shakespeare, William; ***Richard III*** (1597) (1.4) **T**
- [ ] Shakespeare, William; ***Romeo and Juliet*** (1597) (2.9) **T**
- [ ] Shakespeare, William; ***The Sonnets*** (1609) (1.4) **P**
- [ ] Shelley, Mary; ***Frankenstein*** (1818) (2.16) **F**
- [ ] Sherman, William Tecumseh; ***Memoirs of General W. T. Sherman*** (1875) (2.17) **M**
- [ ] Simon, Bob; ***Forty Days*** (1992) (3.14) **M**
- [ ] Sinker, Daniel; ***We Owe You Nothing—Punk Planet: The Collected Interviews*** (2001) (3.4) **NF**
- [ ] Sobol, Donald J.; ***Encyclopedia Brown: Boy Detective*** (1963) (3.14) **F**
- [ ] Solzhenitsyn, Aleksandr; ***One Day in the Life of Ivan Denisovich*** (1962) (6.11) **F**
- [ ] Spinoza, Baruch; ***Ethics*** (2000) (translated by G. H. R. Parkinson) (5.20) **NF**
- [ ] Spurling, Hilary; ***Matisse the Master: A Life of Henri Matisse*** (2005) (6.7) **B**
- [ ] Steinbeck, John; ***The Grapes of Wrath*** (1939) (1.19) **F**
- [ ] Steves, Rick; ***Europe Through the Back Door*** (2003) (3.13) **REF**
- [ ] Sun Tzu; ***The Art of War*** (5th century BCE) (3.10) **NF**
- [ ] Susann, Jacqueline; ***Valley of the Dolls*** (1966) (4.10) **F**
- [ ] Suskind, Ron; ***The Price of Loyalty: George W. Bush, the White House, and the Education of Paul O'Neill*** (2004) (4.17) **NF**
- [ ] Thompson, Hunter S.; ***Fear and Loathing in Las Vegas*** (1971) (2.5) **F**
- [ ] Thompson, Kay; ***Eloise: A Book for Precocious Grown-ups*** (1955) (3.11) **F**

- [ ] Thoreau, Henry David; *Walden* (1854) (7.1) **NF**
- [ ] Thurman, Judith; *Secrets of the Flesh: A Life of Colette* (1999) (2.2) **B**
- [ ] Tolstoy, Leo; *Anna Karenina* (1878) (1.16) **F**
- [ ] Tolstoy, Leo; *War and Peace* (1869) (1.2) **F**
- [ ] Toole, John Kennedy; *A Confederacy of Dunces* (1980) (3.2) **F**
- [ ] Trouillot, Michel-Rolph; *Haiti: State Against Nation* (1990) (5.20) **NF**
- [ ] Twain, Mark; *A Connecticut Yankee in King Arthur's Court* (1889) (2.2) **F**
- [ ] Twain, Mark; *The Adventures of Huckleberry Finn* (1884) (1.1) **F**
- [ ] Twain, Mark; **"The Celebrated Jumping Frog of Calaveras County"** (1865) (2.21) **SS**
- [ ] Vidal, Gore; *The Last Empire: Essays 1992–2000* (2001) (2.7) **E**
- [ ] Voltaire; *Candide* (1759) (2.18) **F**
- [ ] Vonnegut, Kurt; *Slaughterhouse-Five* (1969) (2.19) **F**
- [ ] Waldo, Myra; *Myra Waldo's Travel and Motoring Guide to Europe* (1978) (3.13) **REF**
- [ ] Walters, Minette; *The Breaker* (1998) (5.1) **F**
- [ ] Warhol, Andy; *The Andy Warhol Diaries* (1991) (edited by Pat Hackett) (4.15) **COL**
- [ ] Waugh, Evelyn; *Brideshead Revisited* (1945) (6.16) **F**
- [ ] Wells, Rebecca; *Divine Secrets of the Ya-Ya Sisterhood* (1996) (2.7) **F**
- [ ] Welty, Eudora; *The Collected Stories of Eudora Welty* (1980) (2.7) **SS**
- [ ] Welty, Eudora; *The Optimist's Daughter* (1972) (2.3) **F**

☐ White, E. B.; *Charlotte's Web* (1952) (7.3) **F**

☐ Whitman, Walt; *Leaves of Grass* (1855) (5.16) **P**

☐ Wiggin, Kate Douglas; *Rebecca of Sunnybrook Farm* (1903) (2.22) **F**

☐ Wilde, Oscar; *Intentions* (1891) (3.16) **E**

☐ Williams, Tennessee; *A Streetcar Named Desire* (1947) (1.14) **T**

☐ Wolfe, Tom; *The Electric Kool-Aid Acid Test* (1968) (2.21) **NF**

☐ Woolf, Virginia; *A Room of One's Own* (1929) (1.5) **E**

☐ Woolf, Virginia; *Mrs Dalloway* (1925) (2.4) **F**

☐ Woolf, Virginia; *The Diary of Virginia Woolf* (5 volumes) (1977–1984) (edited by Anne Olivier Bell) (3.11) **M**

Acknowledgments

Much like Rory, I've always lived in two worlds. One is that of enjoying fictional storytelling, be it books, movies, television, or song lyrics; and the other is rooted deep in the factual, wherein I'll spend hours researching the true stories behind my constantly evolving obsessions. I've been lucky enough to carve out a career that allows me to happily wallow in both worlds, and in many ways, this book is a distillation of the two.

An enormous thank-you to my editor, Jordana Hawkins, who let me indulge three passions with this project: TV, books, and absurd amounts of trivia. Many thanks to production editor Leah Gordon, copy editor Mary Flower, book designer Amanda Richmond, publicist Seta Zink, marketer Amy Cianfrone, publisher Kristin Kiser, and everyone at Running Press for their diligent behind-the-scenes—but extremely appreciated—hard work.

My eternal love and gratitude to my exceedingly patient husband, Adam, who kept himself occupied with his own books and television shows during my many late-night writing sessions. Thank you to my friends and family for sharing their enthusiasm and *Gilmore Girls* memories with me; to those who lent me "a room of my own" (a.k.a free rein of their homes while they were out of town) for personal writing and binge-watching retreats; and to my Harshing, Hookers, and ABME group chats for their constant love and support. And last but never least, thank you to Jackie (a.k.a Best Roomie Ever) for introducing me to the world of Stars Hollow many moons ago.

About the Author

Erika Berlin is a disco ball enthusiast, a pop culture addict, and a fan of pretending lowbrow TV shows are educational. She is a Midwestern New Yorker who, like Rory, grew up as a voracious reader (Erika also devoured—and loved—*Anna Karenina* as a teen), and she frequently curates Little Free Libraries in her area as a hobby. She is deputy editor at Music Times and a contributing editor at *Ad Age*. Previously she was a staff editor at *Mental Floss*, *Rolling Stone*, and *Cosmopolitan*, and her work has appeared in *Smithsonian*, *Entertainment Weekly*, Refinery29, the History Channel show *Crazy Rich Ancients*, and various iHeartMedia podcasts, among others. She lives in Westchester, New York, with her husband and two young sons.